Girls with Autism
Becoming Women

of related interest

Spectrum Women
Walking to the Beat of Autism
Edited by Barb Cook and Dr Michelle Garnett
Foreword by Lisa Morgan
ISBN 978 1 78592 434 7
eISBN 978 1 78450 806 7

Life on the Autism Spectrum
A Guide for Girls and Women
Karen McKibbin
ISBN 978 1 84905 747 9
eISBN 978 1 78450 193 8

Women and Girls with Autism Spectrum Disorder
Understanding Life Experiences from Early Childhood to Old Age
Sarah Hendrickx
ISBN 978 1 84905 547 5
eISBN 978 0 85700 982 1

Nerdy, Shy, and Socially Inappropriate
A User Guide to an Asperger Life
Cynthia Kim
ISBN 978 1 84905 757 8
eISBN 978 0 85700 949 4

Parenting Girls on the Autism Spectrum
Overcoming the Challenges and Celebrating the Gifts
Eileen Riley-Hall
ISBN 978 1 84905 893 3
eISBN 978 0 85700 612 7

Aspergirls
Empowering Females with Asperger Syndrome
Rudy Simone
ISBN 978 1 84905 826 1
eISBN 978 0 85700 289 1

Girls with Autism Becoming Women

Heather Stone Wodis

Foreword by Erika Hammerschmidt

Jessica Kingsley *Publishers*
London and Philadelphia

3 9082 13654 3470

First published in 2018
by Jessica Kingsley Publishers
73 Collier Street
London N1 9BE, UK
and
400 Market Street, Suite 400
Philadelphia, PA 19106, USA

www.jkp.com

Library of Congress Cataloging in Publication Data
A CIP catalog record for this book is available from the Library of Congress

British Library Cataloguing in Publication Data
A CIP catalogue record for this book is available from the British Library

ISBN 978 1 78592 818 5
eISBN 978 1 78450 907 1

Printed and bound in the United States

This book is dedicated to the seven women who made it possible. Thank you for sharing your autobiographies.

CONTENTS

FOREWORD

ERIKA HAMMERSCHMIDT

The world and its perception of autism spectrum disorders (ASD) has changed a great deal in the last decade or so. A condition that was once viewed through a very narrow lens, represented in popular culture only by the movie *Rain Man* (Guber, Peters, and Levinson 1988), has become more widely understood as a vastly diverse range of different abilities, challenges, interests, and personalities that is part of, and shades into, the greater human spectrum. Awareness is spreading about the intersections of autism with race and sexual orientation, and, as in this book, the particular issues faced by women on the spectrum.

When I first wrote and published my memoir *Born on the Wrong Planet* more than ten years ago, I didn't realize that I was creating one of the earliest firsthand accounts of living as a woman with autism. I was pleased to see the field expand greatly over the next several years. In my time as a writer and speaker, I've always tried to make it clear that my own view of the autistic experience is one of many, and encourage people who are curious about the autism spectrum to read the writings of many different autistic authors in order to form a more complete picture. The increase in those writings has been hugely beneficial for society's understanding of autism as a whole, and for individual autistic people seeking role models and experiences that may inform their choices in life.

It has been fascinating to see the variety in the stories that come to light as more and more of us on the autism spectrum feel free to share experiences. In this book, Heather Stone Wodis provides a detailed and thoughtful exploration of the various viewpoints of women who write about living with autism.

The issues these writers face are many, and they face them in different ways, forming their own opinions and strategies regarding education, relationships, employment, and other parts of life, depending on the different backgrounds in which their experience originates.

Some of the accounts feature unsupportive parents, some have parents who tried their best but had few resources, and some include those (like my parents) who had a strong drive to accept and support their daughters as well as having the privilege of access to extensive medical knowledge and large financial resources. Some of the authors were more fortunate than others in terms of the social setting in which they lived, from the behavior of their peers in school to the treatment they experienced in romantic relationships.

The autobiographies also span a range of time periods with different levels of societal support, and show the changes that come when society introduces something like the Americans with Disabilities Act (ADA) or Individuals with Disabilities Education Act (IDEA).

This extensive comparison highlights how much difference can be made in the life of an autistic girl, or, for that matter, for anyone, by such factors as parental support, financial means, and the society that surrounds one during those formative years.

Most of all, it highlights the fact that all of us are unique, and when you know one autistic person that only means you know one autistic person—a truth that still needs emphasizing, even today. Although the earliest autistic women writers of autobiography had some things in common, each one provides a different perspective that illuminates the diagnosis from another angle. It is my hope that this book will encourage further writings from a wider range of women on the spectrum, and further explorations of those writings, each one a step toward greater understanding and acceptance throughout society.

ACKNOWLEDGMENTS

Thanks to my loving husband for always being my rock. Thank you to my parents, who have always supported me, and my children, who have contributed so much to my perspective on human development.

LIST OF ABBREVIATIONS

ABA Applied Behavior Analysis

AS Asperger's syndrome

ASD Autism spectrum disorders

NT Neurotypical

HFA High-functioning autism

PDD-NOS Pervasive Developmental Disability Not Otherwise Specified

DSM-5 *Diagnostic and Statistical Manual of Mental Disorders, Fifth Edition*

ADA Americans with Disabilities Act

IDEA Individuals with Disabilities Education Act

LGBQT Lesbian/gay/bisexual/queer/trans

PREFACE

When I tell people that I study autism, they often want to know how I became interested in the subject. So in order to better understand my perspective on autism, I think it is important to share some of the events and factors that led to my interest in autism and the creation of this book.

At the age of 15 I was diagnosed with Stargardt's Macular Dystrophy, a rare genetic form of macular degeneration. There was no history of this visual impairment in my family, nor did anyone else have it. I was told that I would continue to lose my central vision, but that my peripheral vision would always stay intact. I would become legally blind, and most likely never drive a car. Thinking back, I don't remember ever seeing what was written on a chalkboard. As you can imagine, I was not a very good student. My teachers always complained that I wasn't reaching my potential. When my parents asked why I didn't copy my homework assignments into my student planner, I replied that I hadn't seen anything written on the board. Of course, my parents took me to the family eye doctor, but he could not find anything amiss. After several visits, he told my parents that I was probably making it up for attention.

By the time I turned 15, I had already lost a significant amount of vision. It wasn't until my father took me to get my driver's permit and I failed the eye exam that anyone believed what I was saying. I was also severely depressed and suicidal. As if the trials and tribulations of adolescence and puberty aren't already difficult enough for a young woman, adding a delayed diagnosis into the mix threw me into a tailspin. With the help of psychotherapy, the support of my family, and a meaningful trip to Poland and Israel, I eventually began coming out of my severe depression. However, I had a proverbial chip on my shoulder.

After getting the Stargardt's diagnosis in 1992, my mother became my advocate at school. We learned how fortunate we were to have the Americans with Disabilities Act (ADA) passed just two years before, in 1990. The ADA would ensure my equal access to mainstream classrooms in my public high school. But like I said, I had a chip on my shoulder. I was angry that nobody had listened to me about what was going on in my own body, that my vision loss had been dismissed as attention-seeking behavior, and, perhaps most of all, that my grades were poor because I didn't have the intelligence or motivation to achieve academically. Before I began my junior year in high school, I decided that I would show everyone how smart I really was. With access to the materials, I excelled. I enrolled in Advanced Placement (AP) classes and passed the AP exams. I scored well on the ACT, and made plans to go to Brandeis University upon graduation.

I was beginning to feel more comfortable with my new disabled status, but it was still hard for me to advocate for myself. As long as my teachers remembered to enlarge assigned reading and hand me a copy of the notes written on the board, things went well. However, they often forgot because

I didn't appear to be disabled. Without a white cane, guide dog, dark glasses, or any of the other symbols that mark a person as visually impaired, I easily passed as sighted. Passing was an obstacle that made it difficult to get the services I needed. Still struggling with my newly disabled status, I hesitated to speak up when they forgot about my blindness.

The summer before my senior year in high school, I took a job with Keshet, a nonprofit organization founded by the parents of Jewish children with disabilities. I was paired up with a five-year-old boy who had autism at a typical summer camp on the North Shore of Chicago. My job was to facilitate his integration within a mainstream camp group. Early on I discovered my ability to advocate for this little boy, who had limited speech and difficulty communicating. After eight weeks of advocating for Daniel, I felt more emboldened to advocate for myself.

Although I did not solidify my disability identity until years later, I began to develop an awareness of the social forces that keep people with disabilities at the margins of society. I recognized that Daniel and I were both subject to discrimination, prejudice, stigma, and inaccessibility solely by virtue of our shared disabled status. I may not have autism, but I could empathize with the social experience of disability. In addition, I could relate to Daniel's trouble making eye contact and interpreting nonverbal communication. We may have different disabilities, but the results were similar. There are social ramifications for the inability to make eye contact with others; for example, people may regard you as untrustworthy, dishonest, or deceptive if you cannot "look someone in the eye." Our common experience of disability was just one factor that sparked a lifelong friendship and interest in autism. I have watched him grow into adulthood with the support of his family, community, and civil liberties.

Since I first met Daniel, 24 years ago, I have worked with people who have autism in a variety of ways. I have been a teacher, paraprofessional, aide, Sunday school teacher, program supervisor, respite care worker, trainee, advocate, and activist. My passion for the advancement of people with autism is underscored by my commitment to the disability rights movement.

INTRODUCTION

This book is the result of years of research and analysis surrounding the disability we have come to know as autism or autism spectrum disorders (ASD). The bulk of material featured here originally appeared as my doctoral dissertation for the Disability and Human Development Department at the University of Illinois in Chicago. In order to share my research with a broader audience, the content of this book has been revised. Although this edition may sound less academic, the results are still rooted in rigorous qualitative research.

Disability studies refers to research carried out in various domains of academia, including the social sciences, humanities, performing arts, and applied health sciences. It is a scholarly perspective that focuses on the social, political, economic, and cultural circumstances of people with disabilities. One of its core principles is that disability is not simply a medical concern limited to individual people. Rather, the social model of disability moves beyond medical definitions, considering ways in which disabilities are socially constructed, shaped by history, and influenced by the environment. The social model demonstrates how architectural design, mass transit, public education, and other social systems exclude people with disabilities from equal access and participation. Disability studies scholars are equally interested in the deeper cultural values and beliefs that justify and perpetuate inaccessibility, exclusion, discrimination, and oppression of disabled citizens (Couser 2007, 2009; Patterson and Hughes 1999).

The purpose of this book is to better understand the processes by which girls with ASD transition toward adulthood, and how they make sense of that journey. Looking at these phenomena from a disability studies perspective demands a broader cultural critique of concepts such as autism, disability, and gender. Dominant cultural tropes of disability and gender inform the ways women with ASD interpret and tell their life stories; when these narrative accounts are published as autobiographies, they become cultural representations with the potential to influence social ideologies and the next generation of women with ASD. This interactive exchange between the private and public domains is at the heart of disability studies inquiries into autobiography. What is presented here is meant to enhance our understanding of the ways in which girls with autism move toward womanhood, and how they conceptualize this process. This book excavates the variables that affect the lives of girls with ASD as they move toward womanhood through firsthand autobiographical accounts. While I do not seek consensus among authors with autism, I do highlight the significant themes that surface as girls with autism transition out of childhood and into adulthood.

What is autism?

At the beginning of most mainstream papers and books written about autism, authors provide a brief history of autism as a diagnostic title (see, for example, Stone 2005). While this information may be useful to begin understanding autism, this medical history does not represent a complete picture of the subject. In fact, members of the autistic community reject this tradition of defining autism from a medical perspective, as medical definitions of autism have previously been used to justify oppressive ideologies and treatments. Historically, misconceptions about people with disabilities led to social, economic, and political inequality. In his seminal work *Nothing About Us, Without Us* (1998), Jim Charlton describes the nature of such disability oppression and resistance:

> Oppression occurs when individuals are systemati-cally subjected to political, economic, cultural, or social degradation because they belong to a social group. Oppression of people results from the structures of domination and subordination and, correspondingly, ideologies of superiority and inferiority. (1997, p.8)

To avoid perpetuating these systems of oppression, let us cautiously and critically approach the diagnostic history of autism as a jumping-off point from which we begin our journey.

Leo Kanner, a child psychiatrist at Johns Hopkins University, first recognized autism as a syndrome in 1943. Around the same time that Kanner disseminated his theories of autism, pediatrician Hans Asperger articulated autism as a psychiatric disorder in the 1940s. Although Kanner and Asperger are usually credited with the discovery of autism, Swiss psychiatrist Eugen Bleuler had coined the term "autistic" about 30 years before, having derived the term from the Greek word "autos," meaning "self" (Bleuler 2010; Clifford et al. 2007; Davidson 2007; Stanghellini 2001). The connection between autism and autos emphasizes the social dimension of the impairment noted by Kanner, Asperger, and Bleuler, who described autism as a type of behavior or thought pattern characterized by aloofness, lack of social reciprocity and eye contact, difficulty communicating effectively, and repetitive behavior such as rocking and hand flapping. The social impairment associated with autism is still an integral part of modern ASD definitions and diagnostics.

According to the most recent statistics from the Centers for Disease Control and Prevention (CDC), 1 in 68 American children has an ASD diagnosis. Boys are diagnosed with ASD 4.5 times more than girls, and this disparity is not yet fully understood. ASD is found in every racial, ethnic, and economic group. Almost half (about 44%) of children diagnosed with ASD demonstrate average to above average intellectual ability. Twin studies suggest a genetic link to ASD—when one identical twin is diagnosed with ASD, the other is also diagnosed between 36–95 percent of the time. The prevalence of ASD among non-identical or fraternal twins when one twin has a diagnosis of ASD is still considerable, at 31 percent. Furthermore, parents who have one child diagnosed with ASD are 2–18 percent more likely to have a second child also diagnosed with ASD (Christensen et al. 2016). About 10 percent of children who have ASD are also diagnosed with other genetic or chromosomal conditions, such as Down syndrome, Fragile X syndrome, or tuberous sclerosis (Levy et al. 2010). Research demonstrates that children born to older parents, both maternal and paternal, have a higher chance of receiving an ASD diagnosis (Durkin et al. 2008). However, the correlation between parental age and ASD must not be misunderstood as a causative relationship. In other words, the age of parents may not actually lead to ASD. Parents of children with ASD are generally older when they marry and have children because they, too, are on the autism spectrum—the social and communicative impairments of ASD make dating and marriage more challenging, so many people with ASD form relationships and have children later. In a Dutch study presented to the International Meeting for Autism Research in 2015, the Netherlands Autism Register corroborated this phenomenon in which parents with autism of children with autism were older (Buizer-Voskamp *et al.* 2011). This study also reported that parents with ASD of children with ASD were diagnosed later, had a higher IQ, and were more often employed.

The *Diagnostic Statistical Manual on Mental Disorder, Fifth Edition* (DSM-5) (APA 2013) constitutes the modern standard for the definition and diagnosis of autism in the United States. The DSM-5 defines ASD as a range of neurodevelopmental impairments distinguished by difficulties. In a somewhat controversial move, the APA introduced a new term, autism spectrum disorder (ASD), that replaced the old terminology from the DSM-IV where it was classified under the umbrella category of Pervasive Development Disorder (PDD) (APA 1994). The new term measures autism in terms of severity rather than assigning subgroups. In addition to the diagnostic criteria listed in the DSM-5, ASD is often assessed utilizing developmental screening and diagnostic tools, the most common being the Childhood Autism Rating Scale (CARS), the Autism Diagnostic Observation Schedule-Generic (ADOS-G), and Autism Diagnosis Interview-Revised (ADI-R).

Unfortunately, since Kanner coined the term autism there have been a number of damaging ideologies, alleged therapies, and scientific experiments applied to people with ASD.

Bruno Bettelheim's "refrigerator mothers," operant condition-
ing, the abusive punishments prescribed by Ole Ivar Lovaas,
and the administration of LSD to children with autism top
the list of violence and oppression directed toward people
with ASD.

Now completely discredited, Bettelheim set out his theory of
autism in *The Empty Fortress* (1967). Bettelheim, who claimed
that emotionally distant mothers were to blame for their child's
autism, separated children from their alleged "refrigerator
mothers" and admitted them into his Orthogenic School at
the University of Chicago where they were routinely isolated,
deprived, and abused under the auspices of therapy.

Ole Ivar Lovaas was a pioneer in the field of Applied
Behavior Analysis (ABA), one of the most widely used therapies
for children with ASD today, although his original protocol
included compulsory verbal and physical abuse:

> Training was conducted 6 days a week, 7 hours a day,
> with a fifteen minute rest period accompanying each
> hour of training. During the training sessions the child
> and the adult sat facing each other, their heads about
> 20cm apart. The adult physically prevented the child
> from leaving the training situation by holding the
> child's legs between his own legs. Rewards, in the form
> of single spoonfuls of the child's meal, were delivered
> immediately after correct responses. Punishment
> (spanking, shouting by the adult) was delivered for
> intensive, self-destructive, and tantrumous behavior.
> (Lovaas 1966, p.136)

Modern ABA therapists and supporters are quick to distance
contemporary ABA practices from its early origins, but more
advocates with ASD are coming forward with reports of the

punishment and mistreatment they received in the name of ABA (Kapp *et al.* 2013). In my own experience, ABA can be effective only if it is done with explicit consent and the utmost respect for the dignity and liberty of the individual at the center of the therapy.

The 1960s were not an easy time to have ASD. In addition to Bettelheim and Lovaas, Freedman, Ebin, and Wilson (1962) conducted experiments in which the hallucinogen LSD was given to 12 autistic schizophrenics. The ASD community has endured countless acts of violence and oppression including the use of dangerous experimental treatments unsubstantiated by scientific evidence, like chelation, and overt abuse by family members and care-takers. There are even some cases of people with ASD injured or killed in rituals of demonic exorcism (Christopher 2003).

Now that we have addressed the official, dominant view of autism, let us begin to expand our understanding and explore alternative perspectives. So what is the alternative to the medical model of disability that understands autism to be an illness or pathology?

Since the 1990s, individuals with ASD have become more visible in political discourse and more vocal on Facebook, YouTube, and other online forums. Michael John Carley, founder and director of the Global and Regional Asperger Syndrome Partnership (GRASP), published an autobiography of his life experiences with ASD (2008). Alex Plank is founder of Wrong Planet, an online community for people with ASD, and is also a filmmaker and consultant on the FX show, *The Bridge*. In a pivotal moment in the history of autism self-advocacy, Ari Ne'eman was the first person with ASD nominated by former President Barack Obama to the National Council on Disability (NCD). Director and co-founder of the Autistic Self Advocacy

Network (ASAN), he served from 2010 to 2015, and worked to bring the concept of "neurodiversity" to public awareness.

The concept of neurodiversity emerged out of this period of increasing autistic organization, advocacy, and activism. Many people from within the autistic community prefer to understand autism as one type of neurological way of being among others, a defining feature of the concept of neurodiversity. Nick Walker (2014) precisely defines the core concepts at the heart of the neurodiversity paradigm and clarifies common misuses of the terminology.

Neurodiversity is the biological variation of neurocognitive functioning within our species. It does not solely refer to ASD, but a range of neurocognitive styles including people who have bi-polar, obsessive compulsive, attention deficit and a variety of other disorders. Rather than anthologizing these differences, proponents of neurodiversity recognize the value of neurological diversity within our species.

The neurodiversity movement is a cultural movement devoted to accessibility, equality, respect, and social justice for the neurodivergent. Kassiane Sibley introduced the terms "neurodivergence" and "neurodivergent" (see Radical Neurodivergence Speaking no date; Yergeau 2013, 2017). Neurodivergent refers to those who deviate from the middle range that is considered to be normal, and neurodivergence describes the phenomenon of diverging from the norm of neurotypical functioning.

In the same tradition of "nothing about us, without us," autistic self-advocates assert the need to include people with autism at the center of any discussion about them. In fact, many people within the autism community take issue with the group Autism Speaks, for example, because it consists mainly of parents and professionals who may not represent the voices and perspectives of actual people with ASD.

Why autobiographies?

I chose autobiographies by authors with ASD to gain an insight into their life experiences through their own words. Autobiographical writing appealed to my ethical concern to avoid misrepresenting people with disabilities. Autobiographical writing by authors with disabilities has the power to either reconfirm tired stereotypes of disability or break with traditional narrative structures, to "illuminate meanings associated with disability or illness which are invisible when the body is treated in medical terms, through the language of disease and dysfunction" (Mattingly and Lawlor 2000, p.5). Disability autobiographies like *The Story of My Life* (1903) by Helen Keller, *Missing Pieces* (1982) by Irving Zola, *Autobiography of a Face* (1994) by Lucy Grealy, and *Moving Violations* (1995) by John Hockenberry represent more than a single person's experience of impairment; they also reveal the attitudes, social conventions, and systemic barriers that are culturally produced and socially constructed. Thomas Couser, a British academic interested in the autobiographical writing of people with disabilities, reminds us that dominant culture "filters and manipulates even seemingly 'self-generated' texts in various ways, protecting its interest in marginalizing and ignoring disabled lives" (Couser 2009, p.47). Therefore, studying narratives and autobiographies of disability is important because of its interdependent relationship to the prevailing cultural narrative and legal discourse (Couser 2007; Mitchell and Snyder 2000).

Feminist disability studies scholar, Rosemarie Garland-Thomson, articulates five traditional types of autobiography that disempower, oppress, and stereotype disability. First is the biomedical narrative that understands disability as an individual flaw that requires rehabilitation, remediation, or cure. The second is the sentimental narrative that conjures images of self-pity and suffering. Third, narratives of overcoming pervade the genre of disability autobiography; they conform to "conventional narrative scripts such as the triumphant recovery story or narratives of overcoming" (Hall 2015, p.132). Fourth, narratives of catastrophe represent disability as a unique and unusual tragedy. Fifth, narratives of abjection demonstrate disability as something to be avoided completely.

Disability studies pioneer, Dr Carol Gill, explains how the disability rights movement, disability studies, and disability pride are pushing toward a positive sense of disability identity, which is evident in various cultural manifestations, including autobiographical projects:

> These paradigmatic shifts in understanding disability also pave the way to identifying with other disabled people and entering into collective action against unjust attitudes and practices. In addition to mobilizing for political change, people with disabilities are organizing to set the record straight about who they are collectively. They are broadcasting their identities by developing and implementing far-reaching disability awareness education, excavating and celebrating disability history, engaging in media activism, and writing articles, books, plays, and television scripts about the disability experience. Most affirmatively, they are declaring positive identity through disability pride and disability cultural activities, including projects focusing on

the peer mentoring of young disabled people. (Gill
2001, p.364)

The parents and siblings of people with ASD wrote the first
autobiographies of autism, and tended to emphasize the
burdens of disability. Clara Claiborne Park's *The Siege* (1982)
and Dorothy Beavers' *Autism: Nightmare without End* (1982)
portray autism in a primarily negative light as an ongoing
family tragedy. Since autobiographies published by family
members preceded those written by individuals with autism,
they set a negative tone for the public's attitude to autism in the
family. Therefore, the genre of autistic autobiography responds
to negative attitudes bolstered by previous accounts of autism
as a family tragedy or crisis. Newer titles, like Roy Grinker's
Unstrange Minds (2007), celebrate autism within the family.
Grinker's book demonstrates his familiarity with the attitudes
of the autistic community when he writes about neurodiversity.
Similarly, autobiographies written by siblings of people with
ASD are also in dialogue with autistic autobiography. Anne
Barnhill's *At Home in the Land of Oz: Autism, My Sister, and Me*
(2007) and Paul and Judy Karasik's *The Ride Together: A Brother
and Sister's Memoir of Autism in the Family* (2003) reflect more
integrated beliefs about autism that focus on cohesion and
synthesis rather than isolation and suffering.

The first autobiographical accounts written by people who
had ASD were included in memoirs written by parents. Sean
Barron's autobiography is intermingled with that of his mother's
in *There's a Boy in Here* (1992). Likewise, Jane McDonnell's
News from the Border (1993) includes an afterword written
by her autistic son. The number of "self-authored testimonies
of autistic experience" (Davidson 2007, p.663) proliferated in
the mid-1990s. Disability studies scholar Couser notes, "there
have been so many recent first-person narratives by people
with autism that they have been granted, or have claimed,

their own generic term: autie-biography" (Couser 2009, p.5). Building on Couser's work, Irene Rose coined this new literary genre "autistic autobiography" (2005). Autistic autobiography or autie-biography reflects more than personal experiences; it reflects the interplay between the individual with autism and society. These autobiographies of autism fit into a broader cannon of disability narrative and, as such, have the same potential to reaffirm stereotypes and negative constructions of disability and autism or reject traditional scripts of disability and transcend the narratives of overcoming.

Temple Grandin is the most famous author with autism. Born in 1947, she has published numerous autobiographical accounts of autism. Her first personal account, *Emergence: Labeled Autistic* (1986), was co-authored, but *Thinking in Pictures: And Other Reports from My Life with Autism* (1995, 2006) was her first attempt at solo authorship. In 1999, Edgar Schneider and Liane Holliday Willey published their autobiographies. Since then, the field of autistic autobiography has steadily grown. Grandin's personal accounts of autism gained wider appreciation with the release of the HBO film *Temple Grandin* (2010) starring Claire Danes. However, Grandin's experience does not represent the majority of women with ASD—her professional success and choices regarding relationships do not necessarily represent the experiences of other women with ASD writing autobiographies.

Story-tellers learn from autobiographies how to tell their tales. But this is a two-way street. Grandin's *Emergence* was written before the genre got underway, so her self-descriptions are unaffected. Today's autistic child, brought up on children's stories about autistic children, and who in later years goes on to write an autobiography, will give accounts that are textured by the early exposure to role models (Hacking 2009, p.1469).

According to Ian Hacking, these authors were the first pioneers to begin articulating phenomena that had previously never been described. Six out of the seven autobiographies featured in this book come from women of the baby boomer generation, a generation born around the same time that the term "autism" first appeared in the medical literature. These are the first self-representations of women with autism, a condition that had only recently been named and recognized by Kanner and Asperger (Hacking 2009). Therefore, these personal narratives add to our cultural knowledge about women with ASD.

In order to better understand the current state of cultural representations of autism, we must first analyze the origins. Furthermore, studying these first-wave representations of self by women with ASD helps to fill the epistemological gap in what we know about the pre-diagnostic experiences of those born before 1980 (Bracher 2013, p.84).

When I began my research in 2011, I compiled a list of autobiographies written by American authors with ASD using the WorldCat via FirstSearch, an academic search engine accessed through university libraries. This list was checked against Google searches and Amazon listings.

Autobiographies written by authors with ASD

Bemporad, J.R. (1979) 'Adult recollections of a formerly autistic child.' *Journal of Autism and Developmental Disorders* 9(2), 179–197.

Carley, M.J. (2008) *Asperger's from the Inside Out: A Supportive and Practical Guide for Anyone with Asperger's Syndrome.* New York: Perigee.

Cowhey, S. (2005) *Going through the Motions: Coping with Autism.* PublishAmerica.

Grandin, T. (2006) *Thinking in Pictures: And Other Reports from My Life with Autism.* New York: Vintage.

Hammerschmidt, E. (2005) *Born on the Wrong Planet.* Palo Alto, CA: Tyborne Hill.

Holliday Willey, L. (1999) *Pretending to be Normal: Living with Asperger's Syndrome.* Ebrary Collection. London: Jessica Kingsley Publishers.

Holliday Willey, L. (2001) *Asperger Syndrome in the Family: Redefining Normal.* London: Jessica Kingsley Publishers.

Holliday Willey, L. (2003) *Asperger Syndrome in Adolescence: Living with the Ups, the Downs, and Things in Between.* London: Jessica Kingsley Publishers.

Julien, W. (1999) *Carrousels and Storms: Mysticism from an Autistic Mind.* Richmond, IN: Maestro Media.

MacDonald, V.B. (2003) *From Darkness to Light: An Autobiography.* Parker, CO: Paintbrush Press.

Mann, L.B. and Myles, B.S. (2008) *More than Little Professors: Children with Asperger Syndrome: In Their Own Words.* Shawnee Mission, KS: Autism Asperger Publishers.

McKean, T.A. (1996) *Light on the Horizon: 'A Deeper View from Inside the Autism Puzzle'.* Arlington, TX: Future Horizons.

McKean, T.A. (2001) *Soon Will Come the Light: A View from Inside the Autism Puzzle.* Arlington, TX: Future Horizons.

Meyer, R.N. (2001) *Asperger Syndrome Employment Workbook: An Employment Workbook for Adults with Asperger Syndrome.* London: Jessica Kingsley Publishers.

Miller, J.K. (2003) *Women from Another Planet? Our Lives in the Universe of Autism.* 1stBooks.

Narayanan, K. (2003) *Wasted Talent: Musings of an Autistic.* North Andover, MA: Vite Publishing.

Newport, J. (2001) *Your Life Is Not a Label: A Guide to Living Fully with Autism and Asperger's Syndrome for Parents, Professionals, and You!* Arlington, TX: Future Horizons.

Olson, J.K. (2006) *Aspie: Memoirs of the Blessings and Burdens of Asperger's Syndrome.* Bloomington, IN: XLibris.

O'Neill, J.L. (1999) *Through the Eyes of Aliens: A Book about Autistic People.* London: Jessica Kingsley Publishers.

Page, T. (2009) *Parallel Play: Life as an Outsider.* New York: Doubleday.

Prince-Hughes, D. (2002) *Aquamarine Blue 5: Personal Stories of College Students with Autism.* Athens, OH: Swallow Press/Ohio University Press.

Prince-Hughes, D. (2004) *Songs of the Gorilla Nation: My Journey through Autism.* New York: Harmony Books.

Robison, J.E. (2007) *Look Me in the Eye: My Life with Asperger's.* Waterville, ME: Thorndike Press.

Romkema, C. (2002) *Embracing the Sky: Poems beyond Disability.* London: Jessica Kingsley Publishers.

Ronan, T.M. (2003) *Therese: Living with Autism.* Bloomington, IN: XLibris.

Sanders, R.S. (2002) *Overcoming Asperger's: Personal Experience & Insight.* Murfreesboro, TN: Armstrong Valley Publishers.

Sanders, R.S. (2004) *On My Own Terms: My Journey with Asperger's.* Murfreesboro, TN: Armstrong Valley Publishers.

Schneider, E. (1999) *Discovering My Autism: Apologia Pro Vita Sua (With Apologies to Cardinal Newman).* London: Jessica Kingsley Publishers.

Schneider, E. (2003) *Living the Good Life with Autism.* London: Jessica Kingsley Publishers.

Shore, S.M. (2003) *Beyond the Wall: Personal Experiences with Autism and Asperger Syndrome.* Shawnee Mission, KS: Autism Asperger Publishing Co.

Shore, S.M. (2004) *Ask and Tell: Self-advocacy and Disclosure for People on the Autism Spectrum.* Shawnee Mission, KS: Autism Asperger Publishing Co.

Shore, S. (2006) 'The Importance of Parents in the Success of People with Autism.' In C.N. Ariel and R.A. Naseef (eds) *Voices from the Spectrum* (pp.199–203). London: Jessica Kingsley Publishers.

Stillman, W. (2003) *Demystifying the Autistic Experience: A Humanistic Introduction for Parents, Caregivers, and Educators.* London: Jessica Kingsley Publishers.

Thorsos, D.I. (2000) *Sour Sweet: Adversity into Creativity.* Renton, WA: First Word Publishing.

Since the experience of disability is so inextricably linked to particular cultures and historical moments, I chose to limit the list to American authors. I then eliminated books that were co-authored to guarantee individual, "single-voice" autobiographies. I excluded from the sample essays found in anthologies that were written in response to a specific topic, rather than traditional autobiography that fits developmental processes into a wider image of identity. After reading and analyzing the remaining 18 autobiographies, indicated above in bold print, there was still too much material to manage for the constraints of a doctoral dissertation. Based on emerging themes and my interest in gender, I decided to focus on the seven autobiographies written by women with ASD, presented in the table on the next page.

Table 1: Authors' demographic information

Author	Diagnosis (age at diagnosis)	Date of birth	Relationship status	High school graduate	College graduate	Graduate school	PhD
Sharon P. Cowhey (2005)	Autism (46)	1956	Remarried, two children	No	No	No	No
Temple Grandin (2006)	Autism (3)	1947	Single	Yes	Yes, Franklin Pierce	Yes, MS, ASU	Yes, University of Illinois
Erika Hammerschmidt (2005)	Autism, Tourette's, OCD (childhood)	1981	Married, no children	Yes	Yes	No	No
Dawn Prince-Hughes (2004)	Autism (36)	1964	Married, one child	Yes, later	Yes, later	Yes, interdisciplinary anthropology at University Herisau in Switzerland	Yes, interdisciplinary anthropology at University Herisau in Switzerland
Therese M. Ronan (2003)	Autism (childhood)	1956	Single	Yes	No	No	No
Deborah I. Thorsos (2000)	Autism (childhood)	1957	Married	Yes	Yes, Northwestern Virginia Community College, University of Maryland	No	No
Liane Holliday Willey (1999)	Exceptional child (3), Asperger's syndrome without diagnosis (adulthood)	1959	Married, two children	Yes	Yes	Yes	Yes

Why girls and women with autism?

There are many reasons to focus research exclusively on girls and women with ASD. First of all, they constitute a minority within a minority. According to the CDC, ASD is about 4.5 times more common among boys (1 in 42) than among girls (1 in 189). The reasons for this disparity are not yet fully understood. Genetics appear to play a significant role in the appearance of ASD, but the current criteria for autism diagnoses are based solely on behavior; there are no blood tests or physical markers of autism (APA 2013; Baio 2014). Although diagnostics for ASD have been largely standardized, the subjective perception of the clinician conducting the diagnostic tests can play a role in the interpretation of the results (Bumiller 2008). Subjective bias may contribute to the disproportionately high rates of ASD diagnoses among boys and men. For example, clinicians may be less inclined to assign an ASD diagnosis to a girl or woman due to the cultural expectation that autism mostly affects boys and men.

Girls may be diagnosed with ASD less frequently because they demonstrate a different neurobehavioral profile. For example, girls with ASD appear to be more socially motivated and better at camouflaging or coping with ASD characteristics, and when girls are diagnosed with ASD, support may not be readily available (Begeer *et al.* 2013; Brooks and Benson 2014; Hiller, Young, and Weber 2014; Krahn 2012; Simone and Holliday Willey 2010). Further, research demonstrates that clinicians are not asking girls the right questions or looking for specific behavior that would point to the presence of an ASD (Dworzynski *et al.* 2012; Frazier *et al.* 2014; Head, McGillivray, and Stokes 2014; Lennon and Eisenberg 1987; Mandy, Murin, and Skuse 2015). Although more research is needed to clarify the variables that lead to fewer and later ASD diagnoses among girls and women, the issues surrounding delayed diagnosis of ASD are beginning to gain traction in academic and clinical circles.

As neurotypical girls transition toward adulthood, they tend to gain more independence from parents, teachers, and other adults. However, many adolescent girls with autism remain dependent on parents/caregivers for support in education, accommodation, and occupational situations (Solomon *et al.* 2012). For example, they may not achieve important cultural milestones such as getting a driver's license, which, for most American teenagers, is a rite of passage that symbolizes emerging independence and responsibility. I can personally attest to the disappointment and frustration of being denied this. When I was first diagnosed with macular degeneration, I was told that I would most likely never drive a car. Much to my surprise, I was recruited to participate in a study investigating the use of telescopic lenses for visually impaired drivers. After intensive training and practice, I received a restricted (daylight driving only) driver's license at the age of 20. However, I dread the yearly vision examination that allows me to keep my license.

Although girls with autism physically mature at the same rate as their typically developing peers, the social and communicative impairments associated with ASD may impact development (Gabriels and van Bourgondien 2007). Girls with autism physically develop normally, but may act younger, and this gap between chronological age and emotional development often causes frustration and confusion, which can lead to anxiety and depression. In fact, adolescent girls with autism face higher rates of anxiety and depression when compared to typically developing girls. Mayes *et al.* (2011) found a high prevalence of anxiety and depression among most girls with ASD. Girls with ASD, ages 8–18, resemble boys with ASD more so than neurotypical girls without an ASD when it comes to mood disorders like depression (Solomon *et al.* 2012). Their high risk for depression, anxiety, isolation, and mental health issues have been documented in the literature (Martin *et al.* 2008). Another potential issue for girls with autism is access to peer groups, due to segregated or special education, stigma, and exclusion. If they have the opportunity to interact and socialize with their peers, girls with ASD may not have the social skills to form and maintain friendships. Although they may have difficulty communicating with others, they still want to engage in social life and form meaningful relationships (Jones and Meldal 2001). Limited access to peer groups and social networks then affects the type of information girls with ASD have about sex and sexuality. This sociosexual knowledge plateaus around the age of puberty, but girls with ASD may not have the same social opportunities or skillset to develop at the same rate (Griffith *et al.* 1999; Henault 2006; Hingsburger *et al.* 1993; Kelly *et al.* 2008; Realmuto and Ruble 1999).

On a more personal note, my own experiences as a girl growing up with a disability also influenced my decision to focus on girls and women with autism. When I thought about what was important to girls growing up with disabilities, I thought about my own fears, hopes, and dreams. As an adolescent girl with a newly diagnosed visual impairment, I worried about my education, career possibilities, sexuality, and place within my family and community. My goal is not to speak for these women with ASD, but to bring attention to their voices.

CHAPTER ONE

MEET THE WOMEN

I will now briefly introduce the seven women featured in this book. These biographies are meant to provide the reader with a basic knowledge of who these women are before delving into the ways their lives, experiences, and stories converge, diverge, and reveal unique insights that emerge from seven distinct voices of women with autism. For a more detailed account of the methodology applied, please see Appendix 2.

Sharon Cowhey

Sharon Cowhey's autobiography generally follows a sentimental narrative style that attributes the many abuses and tragedies she has suffered to the role autism has played in her life (Garland-Thomson 2005). Sharon was born in 1959, before the IDEA and ADA were passed. She attended a Catholic parochial school, but did not have an autism diagnosis during childhood. As a child, she found comfort rocking in a rocking chair for hours on end. This reliance on rocking followed her throughout her life, and her feelings about it are somewhat ambivalent.

The rocking chair provided necessary comfort, but Sharon also regrets the amount of time she spent rocking. Furthermore, her parents were only slightly concerned about her fixation on rocking, but never followed up thoroughly. During adolescence, she tried to stop rocking, but this resulted in unbearable stress and anxiety for her.

Sharon blames her father for her genetically transmitted autism. In her opinion, her father used alcohol to cope with autism in the same way that she used her rocking chair. Sharon's troubled relationship with her alcoholic and possibly autistic father appears to have primed her for a lifetime of troubled relationships with men. As a teenager, Sharon dropped out of high school and ran away from home with a boyfriend. Running away may have physically removed her from a stressful situation, but it did not solve any of her problems, and only made her more acutely aware of the crucial life skills that she was missing. When she returned home, she was unwed and pregnant. A few years later, Sharon married her first husband—this marriage was to be another chapter in her unfortunate history with abusive and predatory men. Sharon eventually discovered that her husband was sexually molesting her daughter and divorced him.

The next example of Sharon's victimization at the hands of white, nondisabled men led to her ASD diagnosis. Sharon was referred to a counselor to address the sexual harassment that she was experiencing in the workplace. It was within this context that she finally found a word or label for the assorted communication, sensory, and social difficulties she had experienced throughout her life. When Sharon was eventually diagnosed with autism, she was married to her current husband, Barry, with whom she had a son who is not on the autism spectrum.

Sharon was worried about how Barry would react to her diagnosis, as his family had already rejected her on the basis of her unusual demeanor and behavior. In fact, she was very sensitive to the ways others perceived her. As a child, she saw a woman with mental ill health living in an asylum and worried whether that might become her own fate. Sharon revealed the emotional pain that she experienced because the symptoms associated with autism made her seem unusual or standoffish. She was afraid that other people saw her as "crazy," "bitchy," or perhaps addicted to drugs.

Her overall attitude about autism is not very positive—she blames autism for the majority of her struggles, and worries that the stigma surrounding autism will negatively impact the way others view her children and grandchild, none of whom have an autism diagnosis. Likewise, she does not support integrated education for children with autism. This opinion has grown out of her own integrated education, which was integrated not by legislation, but by default, because she was undiagnosed. Sharon's experience was more representative of a student "falling through the cracks" of the educational system, rather than uninformed, unintentional integration. Her attitude on integration, however, seems more consistent with a mother of nondisabled children than a disabled former student. In her defense, Sharon has lived longer as a mother of nondisabled children than as a woman with an autism diagnosis, so her perspective makes sense given her background—her identity as a woman with autism is relatively new.

When Sharon completed her autobiography, she had only recently started thinking about herself as disabled or autistic. At this point in considering her newfound autism identity, she relates her autism to her husband's alcoholism. In a seemingly codependent relationship, Sharon explains how she accepts her husband's alcoholism and frequent DUI (driving under the influence) arrests; in exchange, Barry accepts her eccentricities due to autism. Her marriage to an alcoholic is not surprising given that many children of parents with alcohol addiction also marry someone who is addicted to alcohol (Kearns-Bodkin and Leonard 2008). Sharon achieved her goals to become a wife and mother, but is just beginning to integrate her newfound autism awareness into a cohesive sense of self (Dunn and Burcaw 2013; Gill 1997).

Temple Grandin

Born in 1947, Temple Grandin is a well known woman with autism. Her numerous narrative and academic publications have been widely circulated. Temple's fame, success, and celebrity affords a unique status among the other authors featured here, some of whom know and refer to her. Furthermore, her place in the public eye distinguishes her as an autism representative and role model in a culture where women with autism are rarely seen.

Temple's academic and professional success grew out of personal talent, but the support of her family and mentors was integral. At an early age, before the IDEA, ADA, and widespread knowledge about autism, Temple's mother engaged her in activities that we would now call early intervention. Temple credits her mother for these early efforts, stressing the importance of this type of intensive one-on-one attention that she received. At home, Temple was included in all aspects of family life; she was expected to demonstrate polite table manners at family dinners, play family board games, and attend church, just like her nondisabled siblings. Temple often attributes her success to her "1950s style" childhood, an era typified by traditional family values and social structures along with more formal and rigid social conventions. These rules and routines, Temple argues, made it easier to understand and fit into a world that was sometimes bewildering.

Not only did her mother and immediate family help support Temple on her path toward adulthood, but the efforts of her extended family, mainly her aunt, were instrumental to her personal and professional development. It was her aunt's ranch in Arizona that first piqued Temple's interest in cattle, and that ranch became an early training ground for her impressive career in the cattle industry. Her exposure to cattle and ranch life spurred on her academic and personal ambition, but was also key to Temple's understanding of herself. Further, her passion was a constant source of motivation from adolescence to adulthood. During that time, Temple learned to channel her emotions and control her behavior in order to pursue her education and professional goals. The Grandin family also had the resources and dedication to send Temple to a boarding school that catered to her interest in ranch life and animal husbandry. It was at that school where Temple met another key figure in her life, a science teacher who became a valued mentor and major source of emotional and academic support during college and beyond.

Temple's educational and professional success may have come at the expense of her personal life, however. She never attempted to form an intimate relationship or marry, instead discounting her personal relationships for the sake of business contacts. Unlike the six other women in this study, Temple decided to forego romance altogether, arguing that the symptoms of autism seemed too insurmountable for an intimate relationship. Rather than acknowledging and addressing the sensory, social, and communicative impairments that, for example, make intimate relationships challenging for many people with ASD, Temple abandoned the pursuit of romance altogether.

Temple accepts autism and embraces the concept of neurodiversity, that is, she sees neurology as a range in which autism constitutes another, equally valid and worthy form of neurological embodiment. Neurodiversity envisions neurology itself as a spectrum in which neurotypical people occupy the majority position, while people with autism and other neurological differences represent various constellations along the spectrum. This perspective views autism as another mode of being in the world. Perhaps autism is alternative, but certainly not inferior, invalid, or necessarily impaired. This attitude is apparent in Temple's autobiography, as well as in her public appearances and other speaking engagements. However, it downplays the impairments that are disabling to many people with ASD. When Temple distances herself from disability, she de-emphasizes the mitigating role that her family's emotional and financial support provided. In a time before civil rights legislation, Temple was fortunate to have the resources that made her education and career possible. Without the efforts of her educated, upper middle-class family, autism may have been a more disabling neurological impairment. Temple's attempt to distance herself from disability could be read as a narrative of the abject, because she is trying to avoid the stigmatized identity and negative cultural associations of disability. However, her spectacular success engages the cultural imagination because it epitomizes the most commonly represented literary theme, the narrative of overcoming (Couser 2009; Garland-Thomson 2005; Hall 2015; Mitchell and Snyder 2000).

Erika Hammerschmidt

Born in 1981, Erika Hammerschmidt is the only woman in this study young enough to benefit from civil rights legislation, such as the ADA and IDEA. Therefore, she was the only one with an ASD diagnosis to be integrated alongside her typically developing peers. With support from special education, resource rooms, and paraprofessional teachers' aides, Erika stayed within the mainstream for the majority of her education. Erika's education and self-esteem were bolstered by her dedicated, well-educated parents, who were both physicians and had the financial resources and medical awareness to support Erika in her life's pursuits. From an early age, they sought out accurate diagnoses, appropriate educational settings, and interventions. The efforts of the Hammerschmidts, coupled with progressive civil rights legislation, enabled Erika to be successful in school and in life.

Erika was successful in many areas of school in part because the IDEA and ADA ensured her place in the public education system. Although she was given opportunities to act in school plays and win spelling bees, she could not escape the social stigma associated with disability, however. Erika, like many students on the autism spectrum, was bullied and ostracized by her classmates. She thus presents a more ambivalent image of the pros and cons associated with integrated education. In general, the opportunities and choices ushered in by the IDEA and ADA outweighed the drawbacks of stigma and alienation, but legislation is only part of the equation.

Erika's parents are both pediatricians who consistently supported their daughter's education and creative interests. Her parents encouraged her to express herself through language, literature, and the arts. They had the economic resources that allowed Erika to cultivate her prodigious aptitude for foreign languages, sending her to language-intensive summer camps. These provided Erika with an opportunity to sharpen her foreign language skills in an environment in which common interests outweighed perceived deficits, creating a space where she could thrive socially. In a sense, her differences were lost in translation because everyone was speaking a foreign language. Any lapses in fluency or voice modulation were accepted as part of the process of foreign language acquisition.

Erika is not the only person with an ASD to express a greater comfort within foreign cultures, especially in relation to interpersonal relationships. Stephen Shore also describes how some of his autistic traits get lost in translation when he interacts with his wife who is originally from China (2003, p.102). Erika underscores this phenomenon with a summer romance at a Spanish language immersion camp. Summer camps became a social oasis for her during her teen years, when her feelings of alienation and isolation intensified.

The high school years are generally a time when adolescents are granted more independence from adult supervision and assistance. Erika, however, struggled to assert her independence at school because she had a paraprofessional aide shadowing her. It is not surprising, then, that adolescence was the period in which Erika began to articulate the feeling of being an "alien" or "born on the wrong planet." This feeling, which is also the title of her autobiography, is a double-pronged experience of alienation and "Alien-ation." On the one side, she felt alienated from others in the traditional or existential meaning that social theorists like Marx, Weber, Durkheim, and Sartre pondered. On the other side, she felt "Alien-ated" in the sense of being like an extra-terrestrial being from another planet, the human personification or embodiment of a space alien.

Erika is not the only person with autism to express deep feelings of "Alien-ation;" Temple Grandin also reports a strong connection to the fictional Vulcan alien, Spock from *Star Trek* (Grandin 2006, p.152). Nevertheless, Erika explains how these feelings of "Alien-ation" gradually began to subside, in part, through writing and imagining science fiction civilizations. Through her attention to the building blocks of fictional civilizations, she became more fluent and more comfortable within her own nonfictional human culture.

College marked a turning point in the formation of a disability identity for Erika, where she began to experiment with different ways of integrating her disability into a more cohesive identity. A more accessible environment combined with accommodating professors and compassionate classmates gave way to greater comfort within a nondisabled culture, or Gill's first type of disability identity integration, "coming to feel we belong" or integrating into society. Further, Erika used the internet to develop a vast network of friends and peers with autism, which gave her a sense of Gill's second type of integration, "coming home" or integrating with the disability community.

Erika then met her future husband through her college network of ASD friends and mutual acquaintances. She graduated from college with a Bachelor's degree, but chose to work in a store stocking shelves. Although she may be overqualified for this, Erika stands behind her decision to continue in this line of work, which may point to her evolving sense of disability identity and integration. In Gill's third type of psychological integration, "coming together," people with disabilities begin to internally integrate our sameness and differences. Erika exemplifies this process by weighing her personal needs and desires against those of society, and making strategic decisions to support herself economically and pursue her dream to become an author. Toward the end of her autobiography, Erika's comfort with her own differences and the way those differences are perceived by others supplies evidence for Gill's fourth type of integration, "coming out," or integrating how we feel with how we present ourselves. According to Dunn and Burcaw (2013), Erika also fulfills the six elements of disability identity at work in autobiographical life-writing, which are: communal attachment, affirmation of disability, self-worth, pride, discrimination, and personal meaning.

Far from reproducing old stereotypes of disability and gender, Erika's autobiography is one of the few examples that enters the realm of situated theory. Her narrative fulfills Garland-Thomson's criteria for situated theory (2005) because it questions and criticizes the social, political, and economic forces that mold cultural representations of disability and gender.

Dawn Prince-Hughes

Born in 1964, Dawn Prince-Hughes was eventually diagnosed with autism after a tumultuous childhood, adolescence, and early adulthood. Although Dawn had emotionally supportive parents, they had limited financial resources. Without knowing that their daughter had autism, they could only guess how to best support her. However, they supported their daughter when they became aware of her potential issues. For example, they intervened to support Dawn after she came out in early adolescence. Concerned about the impact of their daughter's stigmatized sexual identity on her self-esteem and social development, the family sought out a LGBQT support group. The challenge of having an "alternative" sexual orientation and an "alternative" undiagnosed neurological condition was very difficult at that time and cultural moment. Being an openly gay adolescent was unusual and highly stigmatizing, but her awareness of this marginal status may have been complicated by the social and communicative impairments associated with ASD. If Dawn had not have had autism, she may have made different choices to manage the stigma and abuse she suffered at the hands of bullies and other unsympathetic peers. The bullying and ridicule she endured in high school due to her sexual identity and undiagnosed autism were so overwhelming that she sought escape through alcohol.

Dawn writes that life began to turn in a positive direction when she found work as an exotic dancer. This somewhat ironic turn of events was only made possible because the establishment where she worked was operated by women who were former dancers. The compassion, concern, and health benefits the owners gave their employees made it a supportive environment where Dawn felt comfortable and accepted. Her job satisfaction was also predicated on the type of exotic dancing she performed and the performance setting. There was never direct contact between the dancers and customers because it was a peep show format in which the dancers and audience were separated by glass, and customers had to pay to open a window and view the dancers. Dawn was successful in this career because it catered to her sensory needs and allowed her to express and explore her sexuality in a safe, supportive environment. The confidence and stability she developed during her exotic dancing career served her well in the next phase of her life.

Starting a new job at Woodland Park Zoo represents another pivotal shift in Dawn's autobiography. Her fascination with the social behaviors of captive mountain gorillas became a looking glass into human culture. Studying gorillas in captivity gave Dawn a greater insight into her own behavior and human social behavior in general. It was around this time that she received an autism diagnosis. Having a diagnosis also gave her a deeper understanding of the unique way in which she perceived the world and her part in it. With support and accommodations from her teachers and university administrators, Dawn successfully completed a PhD in interdisciplinary anthropology at University Herisau in Switzerland.

The personal narrative presented by Dawn perhaps comes closest to neuroqueer-situated theory because of the way she probes social norms, like compulsory heterosexuality and compulsory able-bodiedness (Garland-Thomson 2005). "Neuro-queer" is a term collaboratively coined by Nick Walker, Elizabeth (Ibby) J. Grace, and Michael Scott Monje, Jr., but also articulated by others, like Melanie Yergeau:

> Neuroqueer is both a verb and an adjective. As a verb, it refers to a broad range of interrelated practices. As an adjective it describes things that are associated with those practices or that result from those practices: neuroqueer theory, neuroqueer perspectives, neuro-queer narratives, neuroqueer literature, neuroqueer art, neuroqueer culture, neuroqueer community. And as an adjective, neuroqueer can also serve as a label of social identity, just like such labels as queer, gay, lesbian, straight, black, white, hearing, Deaf, or Autistic. (quoted in Walker 2015)

Rather than adhering to age-old patterns of disability narrative, Dawn asserts a complex and critical standpoint on the various facets of her identity and their social construction. She de-monstrates her connection to a broader disability community through her communal attachment, affirmation of disability, self-worth, pride, discrimination, and personal meaning (Dunn and Burcaw 2013). She also exemplifies four types of disability/identity integration as she gained a sense of belonging within the wider culture, a place within neuroqueer circles and the gorilla nation, the confidence to integrate her sameness and differentness, and increasing comfort with her presentation of self (Gill 1997).

Therese Ronan

Therese Ronan was born in 1956, at a time when knowledge about autism was not widespread. She received a diagnosis in childhood, which put her on track for segregated special education. Therese's family demonstrated a pattern of behavior that did not support her integration or inclusion in most facets of daily life—for example, she was not encouraged to fully participate in the spiritual life of the family. This pattern of exclusion from religious life began in childhood when her parents decided she would not join her peers in the First Communion ceremony, a major milestone in the Catholic Church. Her family continued to exclude her from religious observance when she was overlooked as godmother to her nieces and nephews, an honor that was normally given to an aunt. Therese was deeply insulted that her disability became grounds to keep her from assuming her rightful place in the spiritual life of her family and the church.

Once again, Therese's family fell short when advocating for her education. In an age before legislation ensured the rights of people with disabilities access to an education and other public systems, Therese's education was left in the hands of unsympathetic administrators and efforts made by her family.

Unfortunately, this meant the same type of exclusion that she had suffered in the religious practices observed by the family. Therese's education was inconsistent, both in quality and quantity. She attended at least five different educational institutions, but the ultimate lapse in her support systems was the two-year period during adolescence when she did not attend school or receive any services. Sadly, Therese blamed herself for displaying inappropriate behavior while meeting a school administrator who had the power to bar her from attending that school. She may not have had the legal recourse to address her miseducation, but there is little evidence that her family made much of an effort to find an alternative arrangement.

Therese became interested in boys at an early age, and had a very active fantasy life based on teen heart-throbs and real-life crushes. The depth and details of her fantasy life were quite remarkable, which may have resulted from the lack of potential partners and interference from her family. The Ronan family disregarded Therese's choices when it came to romance to the extent that they intervened to end a relationship—when Therese finally made a romantic connection and they announced their engagement, both families intervened, with the help of police, to swiftly end it. Consequently, Therese is the only woman in this study who wanted to marry but never fulfilled this desire. It seems that her distrust in the social systems of her family and church translated into disdain for formal social services systems, like vocational rehabilitation. She became disillusioned by discrimination in the workplace and poor job training. Although she wanted to pursue a career in the beauty industry, the decision-makers controlling vocational rehabilitation denied her training based on the outcome of her IQ scores.

Despite having an unsupportive family, an inconsistent education, no support from an intimate partner, and systemic discrimination, Therese resisted the forces that tried to limit her choices; in fact, she displayed a critical awareness of stigma and institutional social inequality. In this respect, Therese unknowingly deployed a social model of disability that locates the challenge of duality in inaccessible social systems that exclude people with disabilities from full participation in most aspects of daily life. A social model of disability does not forward the idea that disability is solely located in imperfect or impaired bodies that refuse to conform to the built environment; this ideology is more consistent with a traditional medical model of disability that does not account for the monumental impact and variety of environmental factors, like curb cuts, audible crossing signals, visible signs and audible cues on public transportation, non-fluorescent lighting, civil rights legislation, and an overall mindset that limits the freedom and diminishes the value of people with disabilities.

Throughout her autobiography, Therese referenced cultural norms that devalue people with disabilities. Rather than simply absorbing and internalizing the negative cultural messages about her own alleged inferiority, Therese held social systems accountable for limiting her education, career, participation in religious life, and love life. Instead of accepting and believing in her own inferiority and invalidity, she questioned and resisted the social conventions and authorities telling her that she was not a suitable lover, daughter, sister, aunt, mother, godmother, student, or employee. In this regard, her disability identity played an important role in the production of her autobiography. Therese's critical awareness of the systemic oppression of people with disabilities and resistance to it elevates her text to the level of situated theory

(Garland-Thomson 2005). Therese's autobiography also raises the themes of communal attachment, affirmation of disability, self-worth, pride, discrimination, and personal meaning consistent with a sense of disability identity (Dunn and Burcaw 2013). Her disability identity comes through in the pages of her narrative, as does her sense of "coming home," the second type of integration described by Gill (1997). However, her enduring feelings of marginalization, stigmatization, and discrimination within multiple social systems (domestic, religious, educational, social, and vocational) keep Therese from other types of identity integration, such as "coming to feel we belong." Furthermore, the ongoing and overall conflict between Therese, her family, her religious upbringing, and mainstream society deters her from the other forms of disability identity integration and synthesis such as "coming together" and "coming out" (Gill 1997).

Deborah Thorsos

Deborah Thorsos was born into a Jewish family in 1957, too early to benefit from the IDEA in elementary school. However, she was allowed to begin her secondary education at the local public high school on October 2, 1973, only six days after the Rehabilitation Act of 1973 was enacted. Long before any legislation that granted Deborah a free and public education, her family made her education a priority. Starting with her diagnosis in childhood, Mrs Thorsos sought out early interventions and the best placements available within a flawed and discriminatory educational system. In fact, she played a significantly supportive role in Deborah's life, especially in relation to her education. She continued to comprehensively support Deborah after she graduated from high school. Deborah and her mother even relocated together to be close to a well-chosen college.

The early and consistent separation from peers signaled negative social values about her social status. Deborah's lengthy career in special education appears to have influenced her deep internalization of these messages about her differences, inferiority, and inequality. Her supportive family made sure that she received the best possible education, but this prolonged exposure to systemic segregation and discrimination appears to have permeated her sense of self. In any case, this example of autobiographical life-writing straddles the line between a biomedical narrative and one of overcoming because Deborah measures her success according to her ability to correct or "rise above" the core traits of autism (Garland-Thomson 2005).

Although largely negative, this biomedical narrative of overcoming still reveals examples of a disability identity. Their mutual awareness of discrimination and tentative communal attachment brought Deborah together with her husband Chris, a visually impaired man she met while using public transit (Dunn and Burcaw 2013). Her marriage also provides Deborah with a sense of "coming home," one of the types of integration articulated by Gill (1997).

Liane Holliday Willey

Liane Holliday Willey was born in 1959. In the foreword for her autobiography, she admits that she does not have an official diagnosis, but self-identifies with ASD based on similarities to her daughter. In childhood, Liane was evaluated and labeled as a "gifted student." This label may not have been pejorative or stigmatizing, but her intelligence and early academic success led Liane, her parents, and teachers to expect future success. Liane had friends and was well integrated into the social fabric of her elementary school. However, the arrival of adolescence and puberty marked a turning point at which she began to notice differences between her development and that of her peers.

According to her autobiography, adolescence ushered in the first signs that Liane's developmental trajectory differed somewhat from the neurotypical pattern of maturation. Her autism was less obvious during childhood, when social interactions were simpler. The increasing complexity of socialization during adolescence occurred faster than Liane could process, understand, and participate in new social behaviors. For example, Liane found the complex social interactions involved in flirtation to be confusing and illogical. She knew her girlfriends were behaving differently around boys, but felt bewildered by flirtatious behavior and fashion trends. Liane pondered her differences, often concluding that there must be something intrinsically wrong with her that kept her from assimilating to mainstream social life. She did not realize that these signs might predict a choppy transition toward adulthood.

When Liane left the comfort and safety of her well established and supportive childhood community, she struggled socially and academically. She failed to establish friends and peer groups within the new, less structured environment of campus life. She stopped attending classes because spatial and sensory impairments prevented her from finding them and getting there on time.

If adolescence signaled an emerging awareness of developmental differences, early adulthood solidified these concerns. Looking back, Liane states that she would have made different choices concerning her education if she had known about her autism, for example, choosing a smaller university where she would have felt more able to meet the social and academic demands of college life.

Liane did not know why she struggled through her college education. Despite her social struggles, she formed a romantic relationship while working on her Bachelor's and Master's degrees. Like Liane, Tom, her husband also prefers the company of a few close friends as opposed to large crowds and big gatherings. They both enjoy the format and structure of campus life, so she happily followed Tom to the University of Houston, Texas. After an initial period of successful adjustment, Liane began to struggle with the transition to her new surroundings, and was then unexpectedly fired from her job.

After having their first child, Liane gave birth to a set of twin girls, one of whom was diagnosed with Asperger's at the age of seven. When her daughter was diagnosed, Liane started to see how ASD had affected her own development. Michael John Carley discusses this phenomenon in which a child's diagnosis prompts a parent's realization that they, too, are on the autism spectrum. In his autobiography, Carley encourages his self-diagnosed constituents to seek out formal diagnoses:

> For many people, not having an official diagnosis can prevent them from having the conviction to be able to move forward. Very few people, for instance, go out and spend hard-earned money on books about AS with the same drive as someone who knows they have AS. That alone is reason to get a clinician's opinion. (Carley 2008, p.56)

Liane's autobiography does not correlate to traditional stereotypes of disability narratives, but moves toward an account of situated theory (Garland-Thomson 2005). Rather than overcoming or remediating the symptoms of autism from their lives, Liane attempts to integrate her sameness and differences into a coherent cohesive identity, in an act of "coming together." This narrative also represents Liane's efforts to integrate her newfound autism identity into the wider culture, "coming to feel we belong." Liane may be in the early stages of "coming out" or making peace with her presentation of self, although a formal diagnosis might facilitate that process. Liane's narrative also illustrates her attempts to integrate disability into her own identity and a growing connection to the disability community, "coming home" (Gill 1997). Overall, Liane's autobiography reflects her emerging disability identity based on a communal attachment, affirmation of disability, self-worth, pride, awareness of discrimination, and personal meaning connected to autism (Dunn and Burcaw 2013).

This book compares and contrasts themes that surface as girls with ASD transition toward adulthood. My goal is to illuminate the educational experiences, career paths, sexual development, and social networks that shape the lives of women with ASD. This is by no means an exhaustive or comprehensive account, but a small contribution to the state of knowledge pertaining to girls with ASD becoming women.

CHAPTER TWO

EDUCATION

This chapter reveals some of the themes that emerge as girls with ASD move through educational systems. The first section demonstrates how institutional segregation negatively influences the formation of self-esteem. In the next section, women with ASD describe expulsions from school and early exits from various educational programs. The third section considers the drawbacks to inclusive education and reveals some of the pitfalls that come with integrated learning environments. The fourth section explores how early patterns of escapism continue into adulthood. The fifth section reveals unique coping strategies that enable successful transitions throughout school. Finally, the last section in this chapter articulates the factors that lead to success in college.

School shapes self-image

The educational policy of segregation negatively impacts the lives of students with disabilities (Almazan 2009). Deborah Thorsos remembers how she felt when denied access to the same schools her nondisabled siblings attended. Without the legislation offered by the IDEA or ADA, Deborah had few educational options and little recourse to address her placement in school. In the following excerpt, she interprets the segregated learning environment as a sign of her different and unequal status:

> I felt I was somewhat inferior to them and that was the reason behind not attending the same school. I hated the idea of having to go to a different school from what my brother and sister attended since that made me feel that I was being cast out as being different. I wanted to be just like them and be provided the same opportunities in attending the same schools and making more friends from the neighborhood. It was the idea of attending school for the emotionally disturbed that made me emotionally disturbed more than anything else. I felt helpless in this situation in that I couldn't change the minds of those in charge of the educational system to change for me. (Thorsos 2000, p.42)

Deborah envied her nondisabled siblings throughout her academic career because they were allowed full participation in the neighborhood public school while she was bussed further away to a segregated institution specifically for students with disabilities. Deborah was not born thinking that autism made her different, inferior, or disturbed; rather, these were the implicit and explicit messages that came with her placement outside the margins of mainstream public education.

This process of comparing herself to her siblings became a trend that followed Deborah throughout her education. When she watched her brother graduate from high school, she was forced to seriously question whether or not she could receive her diploma and make a similar transition to college:

> I was happy for my brother to pass this milestone. I wondered if I ever would be able to graduate from high school and go on to college too. I harbored doubt about my future since I was painfully aware that I didn't fit in with my peers due to my social ineptitude. (Thorsos 2000, p.71)

Rather than planning to graduate high school like her brother, Deborah apprehensively wondered whether she could make a similar transition. She was anxious about the possibilities and limitations of being a woman with autism in part because she was not aware of anyone else who had made this transition. Unlike Erika Hammerschmidt, for example, who was aware of Temple Grandin's overwhelming success, Deborah was a proverbial pioneer, forging ahead without a role model to guide her.

Deborah's anxiety about the potential future for an adult woman with autism manifested as a fixation on childhood. To avoid imagining a bleak future with limited choices, she resisted growing up and yearned for the routines and lifestyle of a younger child:

> The focus of my obsession shifted from wanting to be the first one off the bus to having half days of school in the mornings and getting home early in the afternoon. I wanted short school days every day so I could get home early and watch all the afternoon cartoons. I was jealous of the little children who went to school a few hours a day and had more free time. I felt resistance to growing up and wanted to remain a child where I had fewer responsibilities. (Thorsos 2000, p.57)

Not only does this passage point out the segregated political landscape that determined where she went to school, but also how Deborah internalized the messages about her second-class social status. Deborah did not feel "emotionally disturbed" until she was labeled as such, separated from her peers, and associated with a highly stigmatized group of people.

Deborah describes how she felt when she entered the educational mainstream: "I began to attend Theodore Roosevelt High School on October 2, 1973. I was very thrilled to finally go to a regular public school. It felt good to be able to take classes with typically developing students" (2000, p.95). It made sense that Deborah wanted to attend the same school as her siblings to avoid being stigmatized as emotionally disturbed. She inferred messages about her status based on the various education environments she inhabited, internalizing both the initial rejection from public elementary school, and also her eventual acceptance to a public high school.

Deborah remembers how her placement in a school for those who were emotionally disturbed damaged her self-image. She began a lifelong process of comparing herself to her siblings, which started when she was initially separated from them and sent to a different school. Segregation also forced Deborah to seriously question her future prospects. She was concerned that the inequality that governed her education would continue into the future and limit her choices in adulthood.

Education interrupted

Despite the time period and shifting politics that governed ideologies of education, the women in this study did not enjoy the continuity of a typical education. In fact, they often changed schools and programs, having to start over each time. Unlike Deborah Thorsos, Therese Ronan spent two years without attending any school whatsoever. Without the civil rights insured by the ADA or IDEA, Therese spent two academic years, like 1.75 million disabled students before 1970, "completely excluded from public schools" (Almazan 2009, p.1):

> The meeting between Mom and the psychologist ended, and we left. Two weeks later, Mom received a call from the school district. Because of my immature action, the superintendent refused to let me enter their public program. If only I had known what the consequences for my behavior would be, I wouldn't have done what I did. For the next two years that we lived in Pennsylvania, I couldn't attend public school. I do not think that the Bethlehem School District was very fair to me. I still have issues about their not giving me the education I wanted. So, while the other kids were in school, I stayed home every day and watched TV. (Ronan 2003, p.46)

This demonstrates how Therese's disability became the justification for her exclusion from school based on one man's momentary assessment of her behavior. Therese's family did not feel empowered to appeal the decision, and nor did they have any legal basis or recourse to address the fact that her civil rights were being violated. Therese demonstrates how instability and inconsistency in educational environments exacerbated the challenges of transitioning toward adulthood.

Like Therese, Temple Grandin also had her education interrupted when she was expelled from school, but her experience improved when she went to a private boarding school:

> I was kicked out of a large girls' high school after I threw a book at a girl who teased me. High school was the worst time in my life. Going away to a specialized

boarding school where I could pursue interests such as horseback riding, roofing a barn, and electronics lab was the best thing that happened to me. (Grandin 2006, p.120)

Unlike Therese's family, Temple's family had the financial resources to provide her with a private education that supported her needs. Therese was frustrated by a deeply flawed educational system of segregation that allowed a culture of bullying and abuse to develop. She explains how inadequate and misguided teachers perpetuated this culture of inequality and, in many cases, spearheaded the harassment and mistreatment. Therese, with great insight, describes how she had internalized or absorbed the negative messages that lead to the abuse:

My schooling consisted of five different schools for children with disabilities. Some taught only social skills; others included academics. Some teachers were good; some were witches, who would constantly tease and humiliate me in front of my peers. I remember they called me fat and ugly and told me to go on a diet. Then my peers would also taunt and pick on me. They would lie to the teacher to get me in trouble, and the things they said to me and about me sent me into real crying spells. I couldn't yell back, so I took everything they said to heart and cried myself to sleep a lot. (Ronan 2003, p.17)

Therese went to school during an era in American history when segregation pervaded the political landscape and limited the educational options of disabled Americans and African Americans alike. Without civil rights legislation in the form of the IDEA and ADA, Therese had few choices when it came to her education. She was at the mercy of decision-makers who did not have a stake in her future and who were not concerned with fairness or equality for all students. Little planning or thought went into maintaining a sense of continuity in Therese's education, and nor was there much preparation for the transitions from one school to another, which may have been even more challenging for Therese because difficulty in making transitions is often characterized as an autistic trait. When Therese was 12 years old she tried going outside the realm of public education and enrolled at Woods Boarding School with high expectations for improved academic instruction:

> I couldn't figure out why there was almost no education at this school. I begged the school authorities to give me more of an education, but my pleas fell on deaf ears. Now I know that they didn't think that I was able to be educated. I wish that they would have come right out and told me why I wasn't having reading, writing, and history classes, but they kept it from me. Due to the fact that this school was frightfully expensive, I had to discontinue my stay there. I remember leaving school for summer vacation. Little did I know that it was for good. (Ronan 2003, p.41)

Therese was offended that this institution had not been upfront with their assumptions about her intelligence and capacity to learn—their attempt to conceal their beliefs about her intellectual capabilities was insulting. Unlike Deborah Thorsos, Therese resisted many of the unfavorable assumptions about her allegedly diminished intelligence. It seems that she was more resistant to the thoughts and attitudes of other people, whereas Deborah was more susceptible to absorbing the implicit and explicit philosophies that limited her educational opportunities. Therese hoped that the expensive private institution would offer a better education, but the Woods

Boarding School marked another bumpy chapter in her academic career.

Although Sharon Cowhey was born in 1956, the same year as Therese Ronan, Sharon avoided the segregation and special education classrooms that Therese had been subjected to for two reasons. First, she had not been diagnosed with autism in childhood. Second, Sharon's parents had sent her to a Catholic parochial school instead of enrolling her in the local public education system. She remembers some of the nuns using corporal punishment, but focuses more on her personal shortcomings rather than the abusive environment: "Trapped in the world of autism for me was living a very unhappy, depressing, lonely, and suicidal life. School was never a happy time, but somehow I made it to my junior year and then I quit school" (Cowhey 2005, p.42).

In this quote Sharon refers to the world of autism as the place she inhabited and the cause of her misery without highlighting the negative role that the educational environment played in her depression or decision to leave school prematurely.

Having undiagnosed autism was challenging, but the stigma attached to being openly gay at that time compounded Dawn Prince-Hughes' poor academic performance and led to further physical and social exclusion:

> My grades, due to my old problems with people, emotions, and senses, coupled with the verbal and physical harassment brought on by my new status as a lesbian, continued their steady decline... Because of complaints by girls who thought I would "rape them" in the locker room, I was taken out of physical education class and allowed to sit in the library until the end of the school day. (Prince-Hughes 2004, p.55)

Although Dawn did not have an ASD diagnosis, she was still subject to stigma and prejudice based on her unusual appearance and behavior. The social and communication difficulties associated with autism may have influenced the way she managed her gay identity:

> He immediately hit me and knocked me down, He said, "I don't think you heard me right. Are you a queer?" Failing to see why his show of brutishness would affect my answer in any way, I asserted the truth once more. He hit me again. This pattern repeated another time or two. Then the bell rang, he gave up, and we went inside. High school was downhill from there. (Prince-Hughes 2004, p.55)

At the time Dawn attended school, there was still significant stigma surrounding people who identify as LGBQT. However, she may not have been fully aware of the intense social stigma and oppression of LGBQT people at that time. Had she been more aware of the prejudice surrounding her sexual orientation, she may have handled things differently. When Dawn could no longer endure the bullying and abuse inflicted upon her by her classmates, she dropped out of high school. Leaving school prematurely seems to have set Dawn on a path toward depression, alcoholism, and homelessness.

Integration is imperfect

After the landmark legislation of the IDEA and ADA were passed, integration did not erase many of the issues faced by girls with ASD in integrated educational settings (Almazan 2009). Social stigma related to autism is an ongoing problem in American schools (Harrower and Dunlap 2001; Kasari *et al.* 2011). Although Erika Hammerschmidt had an ASD diagnosis, while Dawn Prince-Hughes did not, both recall feeling utterly different from their peers. Dawn spent her childhood, adolescence, and early adulthood without having an autism diagnosis; all the while, she questioned what it was that caused her to feel so estranged from human society. Without knowing why, Dawn still faced social and academic challenges common to students with autism:

> I stood out as a freak in school: my tics, my mono-logues, my sensitivities, my imperviousness to criticism and suspicion of authority, my disdain for connection and avoidance of social interaction, my political convictions, my obsessions with philoso-phy and anthropology, and my odd style of dressing and speaking all led to total ostracism and active aggression. Determined to last out my high school career, I tried to find new ways to get through the day. (Prince-Hughes 2004, p.60)

During her childhood Dawn displayed many attributes associated with autism, but did not know it at the time. Looking back, she recognizes the characteristics or symptoms of autism that cued her peers to her neurological difference and set her apart from them. Dawn not only struggled with undiagnosed autism, but also with the stigma of her sexual identity. During adolescence, the undiagnosed symptoms of autism continued to negatively impact her education; however, the stigma and harassment that she endured due to her sexual identity exacerbated her growing anxiety.

Erika Hammerschmidt was never denied access to public school, but had to endure the pain of labeling and stigma associated with disability. Erika was mainstreamed with help from a special education paraprofessional who went to class with her. At the time she resented the control that her aide exerted over her and the unwanted attention she attracted. Looking back, she believes that she needed that support to stay on task and out of trouble:

> I resented the control. It was worst when the person in class with me had no respect for me, and just ordered me around in a patronizing tone of voice. When I liked the person, it was better, but I still complained that the surest way to ruin a friendship was to put one friend in control of the other. It also bothered me somewhat that I stood out so noticeably from the other students because I had someone following me around. (Hammerschmidt 2005, p.190)

Erika was annoyed because the paraprofessional signified her disability status and kept her from blending in with the other students. She could not avoid the label or stigma of disability because of her visible association with special education.

Erika felt stigmatized by stereotypes of students in special education; she complained that they spoke to her like a young child and assumed she was cognitively challenged. She was badly teased throughout school, which enraged and hurt her. These feelings of being misunderstood during adolescence stayed with her into adulthood. However, Erika resists the negative messages she interprets about her disabilities; she does not internalize messages about her inferiority and worth, unlike Sharon Cowhey and Deborah Thorsos.

The paraprofessionals and educational aides who accompanied Erika to the educational mainstream may have been a crucial part of her success, but their presence also visually signified her disabled status and embodied evidence of a diagnostic label. Like Dawn Prince-Hughes, Erika was sometimes ostracized or bullied by her peers, but Erika had the social support, legislation, and diagnostic label that enabled her to showcase her skills as an actress, artist, and spelling bee champion:

> In addition to being the class weirdo and class clown, I had something of a reputation as the class artist. When my fourth grade acted out Romeo and Juliet—a fact briefly mentioned in the local o'clock news—I was widely acclaimed as the best in the play. The few clips that were featured on TV included one of my big scenes. In fifth grade, when I was in a school that went up to eighth grade, I won the school-wide spelling bee, and placed high enough in the district-wide level that I went on to the city-wide one. By junior high I had gained an interest in how I did in my classes. By the middle of high school I was frequently, though not always, doing my homework without parental encouragement and paying at least polite attention in all my classes. (Hammerschmidt 2005, p.64)

Since the ADA was passed in 1990, integrated learning environments became more prevalent. However, integration opened up a different set of issues related to stigma and social acceptance (Harrower and Dunlap 2001; Kasari *et al.* 2011). Born in 1981, Erika is the youngest author in this book, so she was only nine years old when the ADA was passed, and had more social and extracurricular opportunities in public school.

It is difficult to make a direct comparison between Erika and Dawn for several reasons. First, Erika had a diagnosis while Dawn did not. However, even if Dawn had been diagnosed in childhood, the ADA was not passed until 1990, when she was

26 years old. Although the IDEA was passed when Dawn was eleven years old, without having a diagnosis it is difficult to predict whether this legislation would have had any impact on her education.

Like Dawn, Liane Holliday Willey was also undiagnosed during her school years, but she managed to avoid the social stigma associated with autism. In fact, she was labeled as a "gifted" student as opposed to a "special education" student. Liane's lack of diagnosis kept her out of the special education classroom, and her extraordinary intelligence led to placement in gifted classes; Liane was an excellent student in high school, putting her "on a college and graduate school course early" (Holliday Willey 1999, p.39):

> I was aware that college would bring many changes in my life. I knew the geographic and academics and amount of responsibilities and kinds of challenges would be different, but I never gave thought to how different the social life would be. I had no way of knowing that AS left me without an intrinsic awareness of what it means to make and keep friends, to fit in and mold, to work cooperatively and effectively with others. Most people who come from supportive families learn to jump from their childhood to their young adulthood as if they are on a trampoline. (Holliday Willey 1999, p.42)

Liane ponders how having undiagnosed autism during childhood may have affected the choices she made later in adolescence and adulthood. For example, she may have benefited from the types of support that Deborah Thorsos or Temple Grandin utilized for success in college. Liane was not overly stressed about the prospect of womanhood because she was well adjusted to her primary and secondary schools, had a supportive network of friends, and had no reason to expect major challenges prompted by transition to adulthood. Liane's childhood and adolescence proceeded relatively smoothly; she was designated as intellectually gifted and thought of herself that way. Although her lack of anxiety during adolescence did not require the development of coping strategies, Liane struggled in college and early adulthood without previously establishing these skills:

> I never understood group dynamics, particularly casual friendship dynamics that work on giving and taking, role playing and modeling, rule following and turn taking. Somewhere along the way, I had learned to cope with the intricacies of young friendships well enough to manage one friend. Any more spelled disaster sometimes in very real forms. (Holliday Willey 1999, p.17)

Liane was accepted by every school to which she had applied, and received an academic scholarship (Holliday Willey 1999, p.40). No one suspected that she "needed special counseling or special tutoring or mentoring. I did not seem to need anything more than the typical college freshman needed—a stack of textbooks, a rigorous academic schedule and a dorm room to call home" (Holliday Willey 1999, p.40). Liane felt emotionally exhausted by the time she finally finished her four-year degree after six years. Although Liane did not know it then, in retrospect, it was clear that the traits of autism interfered with daily tasks, like finding a classroom or sitting through a lecture:

> I was aware I should have been attending every minute of my classes and yet, for one reason or another I did not. Though I was not to know it then, it seems obvious to me now that it was my AS behaviors which kept me from simple accomplishments like

finding a classroom or sitting through a lecture. I was
not simply a young college student interested in
going through life at a casual pace without regards
to outcomes and consequences. I think the person I
used to be was unwittingly caught in a game of cat
and mouse with AS. (Holliday Willey 1999, p.41)

Liane's entrance into college was one of the pivotal factors that
eventually led to her identification with ASD in adulthood.
Liane's difficulties in college stood in sharp contrast to her
achievement in school during her youth and adolescence. As a
result, it took her six years to complete a four-year degree
and compromised the way she thought about herself. Sharon
Cowhey, Dawn Prince-Hughes, and Liane Holliday Willey
were not diagnosed with ASD during childhood. Unlike Dawn,
whose negative childhood experiences predicted her negative
adolescent and adult experiences, Liane's achievements as a
gifted student in high school stood in sharp contrast to her
later difficulties in college. Liane was not prepared for the less
structured flow of university life.

Sharon, like Dawn and Liane, was not diagnosed with autism
until adulthood. Unlike the others, Sharon attended a private
Catholic school that would not have been subject to the ADA
or IDEA because it was not a public institution. Regardless,
she could not benefit from either law because they had not yet
been passed. With so many factors working against Sharon, it
is not surprising that she felt the need to escape.

Escape

Integration may have improved the educational opportunities for girls with ASD, but there are still issues unresolved

despite progressive legislation. For example, undiagnosed ASD presents unique challenges for students (Portway and Johnson 2005). Sharon Cowhey and Dawn Prince-Hughes were integrated into their schools because they had not yet been diagnosed, but undiagnosed autism negatively impacted both the academic and social aspects of school. While Dawn sought emotional escape through the use of alcohol, Sharon coped with her anxiety about growing up by attempting to escape from it, spending hours rocking in her rocking chair:

> I preferred to stay to myself and rock as fast as I could, to escape from any embarrassing or painful situation that I would manage to get myself into. Rocking was a constant pastime for me. I rocked for hours and hours, I love rocking. It was all I knew and all I cared about. I seem to do a lot of rocking even to this day I will rock to escape just not as much as I did growing up. (Cowhey 2005, p.12)

The difficulties of having undiagnosed autism may have contributed to Sharon and Dawn dropping out of high school before receiving their diplomas. And although it was unplanned, Sharon avoided a long, drawn-out period of adolescence by prematurely entering into motherhood:

> Running away from home at seventeen was not a smart thing for me to do. I knew nothing about having a relationship with a boy, I knew nothing about what to do in any kind of life's situations, and all I knew was how to rock with music blasting in my ears to escape into my world. Here I am in Maine with a gorgeous thief and I had no idea what the hell to do. (Cowhey 2005, p.20)

Ultimately Dawn and Sharon left high school before completing their education. It seems that both women dealt with the pain of undiagnosed autism by seeking forms of escapism.

During adolescence, the undiagnosed symptoms of autism continued to negatively impact Dawn's education; however, the stigma and harassment that she endured due to her sexual identity exacerbated her growing anxiety:

> [K]ids admired my drinking prowess and the nerve I seemed to have; I would get drunk right on the school grounds. To avoid the abuse of my classmates, I would run as fast as I could to the "drop-point" that my mother's friend and I had agreed upon as the hiding place to leave the alcohol. I would stay there, drinking until the bell rang again. (Prince-Hughes 2004, p.52)

Ultimately, Dawn found escape to be the best way to cope with the abuse and anxiety she faced at school on a daily basis, so it follows that she eventually dropped out of high school to physically avoid the abuse she suffered there. Since she was undiagnosed during her school years, she did not receive any interventions or methods to appropriately deal with anxiety related to autism. It is unclear whether having an autism diagnosis in early childhood would have offset some of the challenges that Dawn then faced in adolescence. In simpler terms, having autism may or may not have played a significant role in the amount of bullying she experienced because her bullies were focused more on her sexual identity than her unusual behavior. However, the unusual mannerisms that Dawn later attributed to autism seem to pale in comparison to the stigma of being gay at that particular place and time.

Effective coping

On the path toward adulthood, many girls with ASD report feelings of alienation and discrimination, depression and anxiety, fear about the future, and sensory overload (Martin *et al.* 2008; Mayes *et al.* 2011; Solomon *et al.* 2012). These are serious issues that require effective coping strategies. Despite the different political environments and subsequent educational system, both Temple Grandin and Erika Hammerschmidt developed creative and effective coping strategies or mechanisms that enabled each woman to meet her personal goals and succeed in school.

Reading and writing helped Erika understand her social environment. The fictional worlds that she imagined and read about guided her toward a better understanding of human social behavior:

> A lot of kids with Asperger Syndrome have a deep fascination with something, and I was lucky—one of my fascinations was language. Besides studying the structure of languages and how they developed, I was interested in anything else that had to do with words, especially books. I didn't deliberately set out to learn about human behavior by reading and writing stories, but that was a helpful side effect of my passion for words. Every time I read about people having conversations, I picked up colloquial phrases, facial expressions and gestures. I figured out from context what they meant, and then practiced using them in the stories I wrote. When I wrote fiction, writing was good practice for social interaction. I also wrote essays about the problems I faced, using words to express to other people what I was feeling. I wrote in my diary to relieve anger and to figure out

how to articulate my ideas, and I wrote science fiction
when I needed to escape from this planet altogether.
(Hammerschmidt 2005, p.186)

Erika could understand the social customs and practices of
her own human culture by creating and contemplating social
behavior in science fiction writing:

As I have become more familiar with the culture I
live in—the human culture—creating new worlds has
stopped being a way for me to escape from the "real"
world and make myself a place to fit in. It's now
just a way to have fun and entertain my friends. But
when I first knew the feeling that I had been born
on the wrong planet, it was a means of survival.
(Hammerschmidt 2005, p.96)

Temple Grandin performed a similar maneuver, in which she
took on the perspective of a cow, and felt comfortable within the
culture of cattle; she then inferred rules about human behavior
based on her understanding of social behaviors in cattle.

In a phenomenon I call the "touchstone perspective," Temple
and Erika both took on the perspective of a culture that was not
human, and this touchstone (that is, cow or alien) gave them
the awareness to better understand human social behavior.
Dawn Prince-Hughes also exemplifies this phenomenon of
triangulating human social behavior based on the perspective
of another outside group: captive silverback gorillas. (The
concept of the touchstone perspective and Dawn's application
is discussed more in the following chapter.)

Temple struggled with increasing levels of anxiety and
frequent panic attacks throughout adolescence and early
adulthood. She built the first human squeeze machine in
response to this increasing and overwhelming anxiety,

designing her machine based on her observation of the calming effect compression has on cattle in livestock yards. Temple's profound empathy with the anxiety experienced by cattle led her to design a literal, physical coping mechanism to manage her own human anxieties:

> I copied the design and built the first human squeeze machine out of plywood panels when I returned to school. Entering the machine on hands and knees, I applied pressure to both sides of my body. The headmaster of my school and the school psychologist thought my machine was very weird and wanted to take it away. Professionals in those days had no understanding of autistic sensory problems. (Grandin 2006, p.59)

Temple developed a key coping strategy during adolescence that enabled her to transfer feelings of anger and displays of violence to more socially acceptable sadness and tears. When she was expelled from school for a violent outburst, she became highly motivated to find an alternative method of coping with anger and frustration. She was able to sublimate, or shift, the emotional energy from anger to sorrow:

> After I was kicked out of a large girls' school for throwing a book at a girl who teased me, I learned to change anger to crying. I was unable to change the intensity of the emotion but I could switch to a different emotion. At my boarding school, horseback riding was taken away after I got into several fist fights due to teasing. Since I wanted to ride the horses, I immediately switched to crying. Switching to crying enabled me to not lose a job due to either hitting or throwing things. (Grandin 2006, p.164)

This process of transference or sublimation of feelings allowed Temple to follow the rules in school and maintain her horseback riding privileges. However, this process of sublimation came at a personal cost; Temple may have avoided conflict or punishment, but her anxiety, panic attacks, and depression increased. This example illustrates one of the key points made by Mandy *et al.* (2015), that girls with ASD have better coping skills and are more likely to present *internalizing* (depression, anorexia) versus *externalizing* (tantrums, violence) behavior.

Successful transitions

Women with ASD appear to make successful transitions from girlhood with the help of supportive families and early diagnosis (Lasgaard *et al.* 2010; Portway and Johnson 2005). Temple Grandin and Erika Hammerschmidt were both diagnosed in early childhood and also received substantial emotional and financial support from their families. Although Temple did not benefit from disability legislation or widespread knowledge about autism, the Grandin family had the financial means to provide her with the educational support that allowed her to flourish and succeed in school. As opposed to Temple, Erika was fortunate to be born after the IDEA was passed; in addition, she was only nine years old when the ADA was passed.

The women who were aware of their disability in childhood and had families that supported their education appear to have made easier academic transitions toward adulthood. Temple's academic success was the result of her prodigious intelligence, support of her family, an environmental structure, and wide repertoire of coping strategies. First, taking on the perspective of a cow taught Temple about the underlying rules of human behavior and inspired the construction of her squeeze machine. Second, sublimating angry feelings and suppressing violent tendencies led to more fluid continuity in her education because she wasn't being expelled for inappropriate behavior. Another set of skills that helped Temple to successfully navigate her way to an eventual PhD was visualizing a symbolic system, such as doors. "During my life I have been faced with five or six major doors or gates to go through. I graduated from Franklin Pierce, a small liberal arts college, in 1970, with a degree in psychology, and moved to Arizona to get a PhD" (Grandin 2006, p.19). Another key component of Temple's academic success was her system of utilizing visual symbols to represent major milestones and moments of transition.

Deborah Thorsos was diagnosed with autism at a young age, and although her education pre-dated the IDEA, she consistently received educational interventions, beginning in early childhood. Since she was accustomed to receiving social support and special education services throughout her academic career, she anticipated that she would continue to need similar help for success in college. Deborah decided to first register at a community college and later transfer to a four-year university course. In 1976 Deborah began classes at Northwestern Virginia Community College, conveniently located at walking distance from her home. Living at home with her family enabled Deborah to build independent living skills in a safe and familiar environment. In 1978 she received an Associate of Arts degree and decided to transfer to the University of Maryland, which was only made possible when her mother moved to Maryland with her. At one level, Deborah had the foresight to realize she would continue to need support in college. On another level, she had internalized the lessons that years of intervention, rehabilitation, and special education had taught her about dependence, ability, and vulnerability. In other words, it is unclear whether Deborah made choices about her post-secondary education based on knowledge and insight or whether she was following the extensive programming and indoctrination into the rhetoric of disability as dependent, needy, and vulnerable. In any case, she graduated from the University of Maryland with a BA in 1980.

Erika Hammerschmidt's childhood and adolescent experiences in public school were not always pleasant, but seem to have prepared her for college life. In fact, she found university life easier than her previous experiences. Erika found college more inclusive and easier to navigate than grade school—her teachers were more helpful and her friends more forgiving:

> When I grew older, things got better. People were much more understanding in college than in grade school. Teachers asked me what the problem was and how they could help me, rather than immediately sending me to the principal's office. Friends were uncomfortable during my insanity, but later, when I said I was sorry, they would accept my apology and seem more concerned than offended. (Hammerschmidt 2005, p.45)

Erika found the college environment coupled with her personal development to produce better social interactions and experiences in college. In addition, the internet was helpful for making friends:

> Socially, college was also easier than previous levels of school. By that time I had overcome many of my social problems, and the other students in college were more accepting than the students in grade school or high school... When I was having trouble

finding friends at college, the Internet helped a lot.
Discussion groups online are a way to enjoy social
interaction without having to worry about body
language, voice tone and facial expressions. There
are groups for just about anything, and I found
ones for several of my interests. (Hammerschmidt
2005, p.187)

Three out of the four women who had ASD diagnoses from
childhood successfully transitioned through their educational
careers, although there were significant challenges. Temple
Grandin, Erika Hammerschmidt, and Deborah Thorsos had
parents who planned for the future and prioritized their
academic success, but Therese Ronan's family did not take
steps or plan for her elementary, secondary, or post-secondary
schooling.

CHAPTER THREE

INTERESTS AND CAREER PATHS

This chapter explores some of the issues that women with ASD face when they consider careers, receive job training, and join the workforce. To begin, I describe how a process that I have coined the "touchstone perspective" functions to help women with ASD find meaningful work. I then move on to reveal how summer camps spark a career interest for women with ASD. Third, I illustrate some of the shortcomings of job training for women with ASD. Another component of successful employment is reliable transportation, so I demonstrate how women with ASD get to work. Next, although women with ASD face many challenges when it comes to finding work, there are examples of successful employment and job advancement. Unfortunately, however, systemic discrimination, lack of job training, difficulty getting to work, and unsupportive supervisors often lead to widespread unemployment or under-employment for women with ASD.

Touchstone perspective

I use the term "touchstone perspective" to describe a unique coping strategy used by individuals with ASD to better understand human social behavior. Temple Grandin, Dawn Prince-Hughes, and Erika Hammerschmidt unknowingly utilized this coping method that parlayed their interests into more comfort and a better comprehension of interpersonal relations. These three women were able to extrapolate lessons about human socialization based on the social behavior of another culture. Temple and Dawn inferred parallels between the social behavior of humans and the animals they studied, cattle and mountain gorillas respectively. Both Temple and Dawn discuss how social behavior among the animals they studied acted as a touchstone or constellation of reference to understand human social behavior. In the same fashion, rather than using animals as her touchstone for social behavior, Erika imagined alien civilizations and wrote science fiction that became a touchstone for a deeper understanding of her own culture. Temple and Dawn based their careers on the unique empathy they felt toward animals.

Temple first began to see the world from a cow's perspective in childhood when she spent time at her aunt's ranch in Arizona: "My connection with these animals goes back to the time I first realized that the squeeze machine could help calm my anxiety. I have been seeing the world from their point of view ever since" (Grandin 2006, p.167).

Temple identified with the way cattle perceive reality because she was often disturbed by the same sensory stimuli that caused the cattle so much anxiety. The realization that there were multiple ways of perceiving reality provided Temple with a greater sense of comfort and belonging within a diverse spectrum of perception. Taking on the perspective of the cattle gave Temple greater insight into the myriad ways that others perceive reality, visual, linguistic, symbolic, or otherwise:

> My experience as a visual thinker with autism makes it clear to me that thought does not have to be verbal or sequential to be real. I considered my thoughts to be real long before I learned that there was a difference between visual and verbal thinkers. I am not saying that animals and normal humans and autistics think alike. But I do believe that recognizing different capacities and kinds of thought and expression can lead to greater connectedness and understanding. (Grandin 2006, p.191)

Assuming a cow's viewpoint was the touchstone by which Temple was able to look back at human society with greater understanding and appreciation. The cow's perspective gave her the intellectual space to contemplate human society from a more objective viewpoint. By taking on a cow's perspective, Temple was able to take a step back from the overwhelming sensory and emotional stimulation of human culture, which created a more comfortable atmosphere to calmly observe human social behavior. The touchstone perspective was not only beneficial to Temple in her personal understanding of her own human culture, but also became the basis for an exceptionally successful career.

Like Temple, Dawn formed an attachment to animals—in her case, captive mountain gorillas. Dawn explained how she came to understand the challenges of housing wild animals in captivity because she identified with the feeling of being a captive animal. Moreover, she came to a better understanding of human social groups after observing the social behavior of these gorillas:

By applying the bodily and verbal language components I had learned from the gorillas, I was beginning to have more social success; this led to less tension for me when I was in social situations, and that in turn enabled me to relax and read people better. This process allowed me to return to the gorillas, knowing more about how human society worked, and learn about the feelings and motivations that underpinned the gorillas' actions and patterns as individuals and as a group. I learned on a new level that communication is meant to convey and evoke visceral feelings, not just rational or mental feelings. Though I had understood what fear and anxiety felt like on a gut level, I now began to understand other, more complex emotions. (Prince-Hughes 2004, p.137)

Although Dawn had early hopes and dreams to become an anthropologist, her career ambitions seemed limited by the challenges of undiagnosed autism, persecution for her sexual identity, homelessness, and drug abuse. However, there is a certain degree of similarity between her childhood dreams of becoming an anthropologist and her eventual success studying animal culture. When she was young she wanted to be an anthropologist because she loved prehistory; it was simpler and there were fewer people. Dawn saw a parallel between early human development and her own disabled development:

I was fascinated with early humans and knew that I would be an anthropologist someday... This was something I could really understand. After all, anthropologists lived among those whose ways of being were totally foreign to them in order to learn more about their culture. (Prince-Hughes 2004, p.46)

Dawn appears to have transferred her anthropological gaze to the culture of gorillas and then related that knowledge back to her understanding of human social behavior.

Like Dawn, Erika became more comfortable in human society through her interest in other cultures. Whereas Dawn inferred lessons about human socialization by exploring gorilla behavior and Temple performed a similar operation with cattle, Erika better understood her own social environment by inventing alternate civilizations in the pages of her science fiction writing:

> By the time I was thirteen, my parents' house was full of my "books," stapled-together sheets of paper on which I had written tales of fantasy and science fiction, of humor and adventure, of children in grade school and people who traveled to magical, secret worlds or met alien creatures. The more familiar I became with science fiction, the more my ideas leaned in that direction. (Hammerschmidt 2005, p.91)

At an early age, Erika decided to follow her passion for writing and become a professional author; she also knew that she needed to support herself financially. Erika decided to seek employment that allowed her to continue focusing on her writing and efforts toward publication. In the following passage, Erika reveals her belief that others have low expectations of her ability to function effectively in the workplace:

> Really, I just wanted to be an author. I had reasoned that few authors make a living at writing and that I would need another job. But I realized that I didn't want my other job to be something that monopolized my brain. If I just stocked shelves for a living, for example, I could devote most of my thinking to the

ideas that really fascinated me. I didn't mind that a job like that would pay less than translating... I work about forty hours a week, and I do surprisingly well. There are "stresses," but seldom anything that sends me into panic attacks or sensory overload. (Hammerschmidt 2005, p.137)

Rather than focusing mainly on her education and career at the expense of other facets of life, she strove for greater balance. Erika's passion and aspiration to become an author was not the only factor that motivated her throughout childhood and adulthood; she was also motivated by friendship and romance.

Temple may have utilized the touchstone perspective to advance a stellar career, but she did so at the expense of interpersonal relationships. Realizing long ago that intimate friendships and potential romance were overwhelming and difficult, Temple channeled those energies toward her career instead. Temple and Dawn developed careers based on their unique insights into animal behavior. Temple's route was more direct, but she had several advantages in this regard. For example, she had a diagnosis from early childhood, whereas Dawn was not diagnosed until well into her adulthood. She then suffered a long detour that led away from fulfilling her professional goals without a diagnosis and appropriate social supports; she dropped out of school and became homeless until she began working at Woodland Park Zoo.

Like Temple, Erika discovered her passion for creative writing and science fiction in childhood, but she had been born in a different era in which she had more opportunities. Unlike Temple, Erika had the benefit of attending school during a time when integration was legally mandated by the IDEA and ADA, so participation in all components of the school day allowed her to pursue multiple interests, like art and acting. Temple, on the other hand, was not legally guaranteed any education, but had to rely on the strong support of her family to ensure a good education. It seems logical that the extra energy it took Temple to justify and maintain access to an education diminished the time she had to socialize and discover other interests. In order to succeed at that time, it appears that Temple had to focus on her education and career at the expense of other facets of life, like friendships and romance. In any case, the phenomenon of the touchstone perspective may be a useful concept to help other individuals with autism who are eager to better understand social interactions and meaning. This concept also reinforces the efficacy of supporting girls with ASD as they pursue their passions and develop strategies that incorporate these findings regarding the touchstone perspective.

Summer camp sparks career interests

Summer camps offer opportunities for girls with ASD to socialize and develop interests outside of school (Goodwin and Staples 2005). At these camps, Deborah Thorsos discovered a passion for art and Erika Hammerschmidt developed her love for foreign languages and culture in language immersion camps. However, their respective artistic and linguistic talents could not be harnessed for a future career.

Although Erika decided to pursue her ambitions to become an author, writing was not her only interest or talent; she also had a passion and proclivity for foreign languages. Erika honed her fluency in several different languages at immersion summer camps throughout her childhood and adolescence.

She rejected the idea that she needed a high-paying or prestigious job to signify success; she was content to work in a stockroom for a decent wage and health benefits while she worked toward her primary goal to become a published author. Coincidently, she achieved her professional goals by publishing the autobiography featured in this research.

> Every summer, from the year I was seven until the year I was eighteen, I went to language camp. I had learned German at the same time I learned my mother tongue of English, so it began with Waldsee, the Concordia Language Villages' German camp in Bemidji, Minnesota. Later I added Spanish to my repertoire, and started going to the same organization's Spanish camps in various sites. Early on, I took two-week sessions, and later four week sessions, sometimes more than one a year. (Hammerschmidt 2005, p.117)

Erika thought about harnessing her aptitude for foreign language for the purposes of a career as a translator, but this career path was not well planned and never came to fruition:

> As a kid, I had wanted to be a translator. The more I found out about that occupation, however, the less attractive it seemed to me. I had been interested in written translating, not spoken interpreting; I didn't feel I had the mental reflexes to think on my feet as fast as would be required. But written translating seemed a lot like schoolwork. I imagined every day would be a battle with my willpower, trying to force myself to sit down and do the day's assignments, the way I had struggled with homework in school. As with my homework, I could probably have done it well, but I wouldn't enjoy it. Furthermore, I couldn't find any

translating services that would hire someone without
a special degree in translation. (Hammerschmidt
2005, p.136)

In retrospect, Erika was not upset that a career as a translator
never materialized because her primary goal was to become
an author.

Like Erika, Deborah Thorsos also attended summer camps
that offered opportunities for self-expression and discovery.
At camp, Deborah pursued her passion for art. When she was
absorbed in artistic endeavors, her autistic identity took a back
seat to her identity as an artist: "When I worked on my art, I
was like any other artist with or without autism. During the
moment it was as if I didn't have autism, I was just an artist
pursuing art. For the time being I was like anyone else in my
art classes" (Thorsos 2000, p.126).

Deborah could not pursue a career in the arts due to
limitations in vocational training, transportation, and general
support. She never aspired to work in a cafeteria during her
youth, but that was one of the few career paths open to her.
Despite a college education, passion for art, and desire to work
with other disabled people, Deborah was limited by lack of
opportunity and training, employers' assumptions about her
abilities, and the pressure to avoid being financially dependent
on her family.

For Erika and Deborah, summer camps presented more
opportunities for self-expression, socialization, and developing
talents. Although they were unable to transfer their respective
passion for art and foreign language into career paths, they
still gained crucial social skills and exposure to peers. Since
summer camps were such a positive experience for Erika and
Deborah, it stands that other girls with autism could also benefit
from similar recreational opportunities outside of school.

Job training

Vocational rehabilitation services have a role to play in the career development of women with ASD. Contemporaries Therese Ronan, born in 1956, and Deborah Thorsos, born in 1957, were unsatisfied with the job training they received. Therese was not allowed to pursue her professional interests or to make decisions about the type of vocational rehabilitation she received. Although Deborah had a Bachelor's degree, passion for art, and interest in working with people who had disabilities, she was trained in a sheltered workshop and subsequently became a cafeteria worker.

Erika Hammerschmidt represents a younger generation of women with autism: born in 1981, she received less formal vocational training, but was still limited to menial work in a stockroom. Erika, however, was satisfied with her employment because it gave her the time and energy to focus on becoming a published author.

Therese received job training for menial work in high school, which was not helpful for job advancement: "I was trained to do restaurant clean-up work and other janitorial jobs that didn't allow me to get ahead in the workforce. I later found out that I would never get any jobs other than clean up in public restaurants—at least not for a while" (Ronan 2003, p.50). Therese was not interested in janitorial work; she wanted a career in the beauty industry, but was denied this based on her IQ score. Although the vocational rehabilitation she received would help her find a job, she was disappointed:

> The transition from high school to the real work world was exciting at first. But then I was naive about trusting that the vocational rehabilitation people would someday find me a more suitable employment situation. Bah humbug! I lived in my parents' house

during this time. I joined a workshop for a while. One
day, I called the workshop and lied to them. "I have
a new job," I said, because after several months of
the extended promise that they would find me a job,
I decided that I'd had it with them. (Ronan 2003, p.53)

Therese was repeatedly disappointed by the vocational
rehabilitation she was offered, but more let down by the services
she did not receive. She had hoped vocational rehabilitation
would advance her career, but she had been told her IQ was
not high enough:

I went through rehab for job advancement. I expressed
the sincere desire to attend beauty school and would
have graduated from beauty school with flying colors.
Nevertheless, I didn't score well on my IQ tests, and
vocational rehabilitation people decided they really
didn't have the funds for me to attend. Folks like that
put way too much emphasis on IQ scores and not
nearly enough on how much more the person who has
developmental delays is really capable of. In other
words, the dis is always put before the abilities. And
it's only because of our labels that we are denied the
jobs that we deserve as much as a so-called normal
person. (Ronan 2003, p.124)

Erika had little formal job training or vocational rehabilitation.
She was not offered services via public school, but had some
assistance from a private job counselor. She had not found the
job counselor services to be crucial to her job search:

The job-searching process was a lot of work, and I
got some help from a job counselor that my mom had
found. The job counselor mainly explained things
like how to put together a resume and how to fill out

applications. When I got a job, I felt that I probably would have been able to do it without that help, but the help sure made it a lot easier. (Hammerschmidt 2005, p.136)

If Erika had had better job training, she might have been able to pursue her career aspirations more effectively. Perhaps earlier vocational rehabilitation services could have been employed to help Erika apply her vast foreign language skills to the job market or discover more direct routes to authorship.

When Deborah Thorsos first switched to a new school, she was hopeful that it would help her learn job skills that could further her career ambitions. At the very least, the Adams School provided her with a tangible transition toward adulthood because she earned money and practiced utilizing public transit independently for the first time:

I liked the idea of doing things for money, though I never had had summer or after-school jobs. Even the transportation seemed like I was going to and from a real job. I commuted both ways on the subway. It was much easier than going to my other school. (Thorsos 2000, p.91)

Deborah, however, was disappointed by the job training she actually received courtesy of the Adams School. Rather than building on her strengths and interests, she found herself in a sheltered workshop environment:

I was interested in learning practical skills that I could possibly apply in the job market. The Adams School made contracts with several of the area's businesses to provide repetitive jobs for the students in a sheltered workshop-like setting. About thirty adolescents including myself met for an hour a day

in a large room, where tables were set up for basic
tasks, primarily packaging things such as emery
boards and plastic covers for record albums. We were
each paid piece-meal rates, which came out less than
minimum wage. (Thorsos 2000, p.90)

Deborah thus revealed the limited employment reality for a
woman with a developmental disability at that particular
time and place. Rather than considering her talents and
skills for a rewarding career, she was relegated to menial
labor for less than the minimum wage. Furthermore, having
her career aspirations squelched by vocational rehabilitation
compromised the confidence she had to assert her will and
pursue her own interests. Deborah's experience highlights a
widely held social attitude that adolescents with developmental
disabilities will never develop into fully-fledged adults. The
system perpetuated her dependence on others and limited her
choices. In this way, Deborah was denied the American values
of independence and liberty.

Unlike Deborah, Erika had very little job experience during
adolescence. Although Deborah had grown up in a different
era and received vocational training, both women graduated
from college in similar predicaments and struggled to find
employment:

After graduating from college, it took me a long
time to find a job that paid enough for me to live on.
I had worked a little bit before graduating—I had put
textbooks on shelves in the store at my college, and I
had volunteered doing odd jobs for a co-op and a little
acting group. In all those jobs, I had been preoccupied
with what people thought of me; I had been haunted
by a constant fear that maybe I was doing things
wrong and the managers didn't like me. I also didn't

trust my own work ethic very much; every place I had
worked, I had found myself being somewhat lazy, not
trying hard enough to find things to do. So I was quite
scared of having a job I would depend on for the basic
necessities of life. (Hammerschmidt 2005, p.135)

When Erika began her job search after graduating from college,
she had little previous experience or formal support from
vocational rehabilitation. In the above passage she reveals
how the social, interpersonal component of the workplace was
more troublesome than the actual work itself. At that point
she did not have much confidence in her ability to adequately
perform her job duties, and nor did she have the confidence
in her ability to effectively work with others. This once again
begs the question of whether or not more job training, relevant
experience, and formal support would have given Erika a
greater sense of confidence as an employee and coworker.

Despite the fact that Deborah and Erika were born in different
eras, both women with autism graduated from college, a major
milestone that often signifies a transition toward adulthood, and
they both struggled to find meaningful employment afterward.
Instead of receiving vocational training, Deborah was confined
to a sheltered workshop that did not prepare her for future
employment.

Getting to work

Sensory and perceptual differences pose unique challenges
for women with ASD when accessing public transport or
driving a vehicle. The only two women in this study who have
driver's licenses are Liane Holliday Willey and Temple Grandin.

Although Temple acquired a driver's license, she recalls the sensory difficulties that made driving a challenge. Deborah Thorsos took driver's education courses through high school, but was unable to pass the road test. She was excited, however, to use public transport on her own because it signified a major step toward independence and adulthood.

In order to pursue her career, Temple needed to drive a car, or more specifically, a pickup truck. In the mostly rural, male-dominated world of ranching, public transport was not an option. Temple's motivation to succeed in her career was so strong that she was willing to put in the extra time and attention it took to master driving a car. As in other facets of her life, Temple was highly motivated by her career and put most of her energy toward that end:

> Often I am asked how I can drive if I cannot multitask. I can drive because the operation of the car, steering and braking, has become a fully automatic skill. Research has shown that when a motor skill is first being learned, one has to consciously think about it. When the skill becomes fully learned, the frontal cortex is no longer activated and only the motor parts of the brain are turned on. I learned to drive on ranch roads in Arizona and I did not drive on the freeway or in heavy traffic for a full year. This avoided the multitasking issue because when I finally started driving in traffic, my frontal cortex was able to devote all its processor space to watching traffic. I recommend that people on the spectrum who are learning to drive spend up to a year driving on easy roads until steering, braking, and other car operations can be done without conscious thought. (Grandin 2006, p.118)

Temple thus attributes the challenge of driving with autism to difficulties with motor planning and multitasking. She was able to manage the challenge of learning to drive by understanding how her brain processed motor information, which required considerable practice.

Liane Holliday Willey, who also drives, identified with ASD later in life, so there was nothing to suggest that driving would be a challenge. She did not anticipate having trouble driving or how it would impact her career:

> Everything about my job was darn near perfect, except for one crippling element—the school's physical location. Unfortunately, the campus I worked on was located in a terribly busy and overcrowded urban area; a nightmare I had to contend with day in and day out. I was never able to find my way to school without first getting lost in some capacity; be it driving the wrong way down a one-way street or missing my exits or following the wrong detours. To make matters worse, I drove a mini-station wagon that did not have an automatic transmission or air conditioning; in other words, a vehicle that did very little to comfort me in the hot and humid Houston weather. All these elements forced my sensory integration dysfunction into a high state of chaos. Without fail, I would arrive at the university sweating, sticky, anxious, dazed and confused. Luckily, my interest in teaching students and the college campus environment usually carried me beyond the brink, so that after my sensory systems defrosted, I completely loved my job. (Holliday Willey 1999, p.52)

In a general way, Liane explores the same issues that Temple raises—sensory overload and difficulty with motor planning—

but without using scientific language. Liane knew driving was stressful, but because she was not diagnosed, she did not know why it was so challenging.

Liane enjoyed her first job after college, but did not anticipate how getting to her job would affect her performance—while she was very satisfied with her work, she did not realize how her commute would impact her ability to successfully function in the workplace. Although she may not have realized the extent to which transport affected her job performance, her employers were acutely aware, and it eventually cost her a job that she enjoyed.

Like other teens, Deborah Thorsos looked forward to the independence signified by attaining a driver's license, so she enrolled in driver's education at her school. However, the sensory overload that Temple and Liane described was too overwhelming for Deborah, and she failed her road test:

> As part of my high school curriculum, I took driver's education offered at the school, which included both classroom and on the road instruction. I thought it was good for me to learn how to drive, even though I didn't have plans to get a car soon, just in case I would need to for my independence. (Thorsos 2000, p.108)

Unlike Temple who needed a driver's license to further her career, Deborah lived in an urban setting where driving was not necessary to ensure her employment or independence later in life:

> That was the last time I drove anywhere. After my mother told me that many people flunk their driver's test the first time too, I didn't feel so bad about my failure. I realized that I didn't need a license since

I didn't feel that I would drive anyway. (Thorsos 2000, p.109)

Although Deborah felt reassured that a driver's license was not critical to her independence, this lack ultimately limited her employment opportunities:

I hooked up with an agency that specialized in services for those with challenges, the Resources for the Handicapped based in Bothell, a community on the northern shore of Lake Washington. Through that agency I was sent to a few job interviews for live-in attendant care for people with various physical disabilities. I was turned down because they needed someone with a car and who could drive. (Thorsos 2000, p.179)

Deborah was kept from pursuing a career working with other people who had disabilities in part because she lacked a driver's license. The job opportunities open to her were not only limited by stereotypes pertaining to the skills of disabled employees, but further limited by access to transport via a driver's license. If Deborah had lived in a rural setting like Temple, where she could practice on open country roads for a long period of time, she would have been more motivated to attain a license. However, she made peace with her reliance on public transit and eventually came to see the benefits, especially after meeting her future husband on a public bus.

Driving a car can be an overwhelming sensory and cognitive processing experience for women with ASD. Temple made a major effort to learn how to drive, and it took years of practice. Liane achieved the rite of passage that a driver's license represents in American culture, but did not know why driving caused her so much anxiety and confusion. Temple and Liane utilized driver's licenses to pursue their career goals, while Deborah illustrated how her career suffered because she could not drive.

Job advancement and successful employment

This section explores some of the variables that help women with ASD find work, keep a job, and excel in the workplace. Although Erika Hammerschmidt was over-qualified, she was satisfied with the highly structured environment and clear feedback that her job in the stockroom offered. Deborah Thorsos and Temple Grandin, on the other hand, did not fully recognize the role that the external environment played in their career paths; rather, they tended to emphasize their personal efforts to succeed. In this way, they typify the overcoming narrative so common in autobiographies of disability. Temple may have focused more on her own endeavors to succeed in the workplace rather than environmental factors, but readily admits that role models and mentors were crucial for her success:

> Luckily, the work is very structured, and it's usually very clear what I'm supposed to do, so I don't find myself being lazy for lack of an obvious task to carry out. My "performance numbers" always show that my performance is excellent. All in all, it's working out fairly well. Someday I'd love to become as successful as an author that I don't need another job, but until then, my job will be in the stockroom. (Hammerschmidt 2005, p.138)

Although Deborah was initially content working behind the scenes, she eventually expressed a desire to work directly with customers. She felt she benefited from more exposure to other people and social situations where she could hone her social skills through daily practice. Deborah credits an improved personal appearance and social fluency for job advancement:

> My prayer of working out in the front serving people directly was answered. During the lunch service hours, I was assigned to serve on a hot food line where I was in direct contact with customers. Apparently, the managers began to feel more comfortable to have me face the patrons and provide direct service as my more autistic facial and bodily expressions had gradually given way to a more outgoing look. (Thorsos 2000, p.260)

Deborah accepted the rationale that her personal appearance and mannerisms associated with autism were too inappropriate for interfacing with customers. Rather than criticize the system that was inaccessible and prejudiced against her, she focused on her personal defects and strengths.

Like her contemporary Deborah, Temple also emphasized her individual gains and personal choices rather than exclusive employment practices within a discriminatory system:

> I still remember taking that vital first step in establishing my credibility in the livestock industry. I knew if I could get an article published in the *Arizona Farmer Ranchman*, I could go on from there. While I was attending a rodeo, I walked up to the publisher of the magazine and asked him if he would be interested in an article on the design of squeeze chutes. He said he would be, and the following week I sent in

an article entitled "The Great Headgate Controversy." It discussed the pros and cons of different types of chutes. Several weeks later I received a call from the magazine; they wanted to take my picture at the stockyards. I just could not believe it. It was plain old nerve that got me my first job. That was in 1972. From then on I wrote for the magazine regularly while I was working on my Master's degree. (Grandin 2006, p.112)

Temple demonstrated a pattern of thought and reactions to professional situations that emphasized her actions rather than systemic patterns of exclusion or primary support roles played by helpful coworkers:

I quit the job at Corral Industries and continued to write for the *Arizona Farmer Ranchman* while I started my design business on a freelance basis. Freelancing enabled me to avoid many of the social problems that can occur at a regular job. It meant I could go in, design a project, and leave before I got into social difficulties. I still don't easily recognize subtle social cues for trouble, though I can tell a mile away if an animal is in trouble. When a new manager took over the *Arizona Farmer Ranchman*, I did not realize that he thought I was weird and I was in danger of being fired. A fellow employee told me that he was turned off by me. My pal Susan saw the warning signs, and she helped me assemble a portfolio of all my articles. After the manager saw how many good articles I had written, he gave me a raise. This experience taught me that to sell my services to clients; I always had to have a portfolio of drawings and photos of completed projects. I learned

> to avoid social problems by limiting my discussions
> with clients to technical subjects and avoiding gossip
> about the social life of the people I worked with.
> (Grandin 2006, p.114)

The irony of the situation captured in the above excerpt is that Temple's job was saved because a friendly coworker intervened, but she still could not see the importance of nurturing workplace friendships. In contrast, she came away from this scenario with the message to further limit social interactions in the workplace.

Contrary to Deborah and Temple, Dawn Prince-Hughes recognizes the impact that supportive coworkers and supervisors had on her job satisfaction. Despite the nature of the work, Dawn found exotic dancing to be a positive and empowering job because of the environment and the people who worked there. It was not Dawn's childhood ambition to become an exotic dancer, but it was a major step toward stability and reintegration into social life after years of homelessness and drug abuse:

> Our dancing establishment, called the Amusement
> Center, was unique as a business. To start with, it
> had glass all around the stage so no one could touch
> the dancers. Visitors dropped quarters into a meter
> to get a screen to go up, for about twenty seconds a
> quarter. More important, though, the establishment
> was managed by women who were themselves
> dancers and knew the grueling demands of the work.
> (Prince-Hughes 2004, p.72)

Unlike Temple who received an autism diagnosis in early childhood, Dawn was not diagnosed with autism until later in her adulthood. There was no expectation that Dawn might require early interventions or ongoing social support to guide her into adulthood, so she fell through the proverbial cracks in the educational system and became homeless, addicted to alcohol, and deeply depressed.

Temple may have downplayed the crucial role that friends and coworkers had on her professional development, but she never hesitates to stress the importance of role models and mentors in her professional life. Temple realizes that role models were an essential part of her academic and professional success:

> I was a miserable, bored student and I did not study until I was mentored by Mr Carlock, my high school science teacher. Over the years I have observed that the high-functioning autistic individuals who became successful have had two important factors in their lives: mentoring and the development of talents. The students who failed to have a good career often had no mentors and no development of their talents. I ended up in a career where I could use my visual skills to design cattle-handling facilities. (Grandin 2006, p.116)

Temple reiterates how important it was to have understanding mentors and role models who valued her unique talents and strove to guide her toward success:

> I learned how to draw engineering design by closely watching a very talented draftsman when we worked together at the same feed yard construction company. David was able to render the most fabulous drawings effortlessly. After I left the company, I was forced to do all my own drawing. By studying David's drawings for many hours and photographing them in my memory I was actually able to emulate David's drawing style. (Grandin 2006, p.13)

While Temple was grateful for help at work, she may not have fully appreciated how critical friendships, coworkers, and other relationships were to her professional success.

Environmental factors such as the structure of work, social biases toward people with disabilities, helpful coworkers, positive role models, and supportive employers play a key role in the careers paths of women with autism. Personal will and ambition certainly seem significant, but the built environment and social norms also affect the potential for women with autism to succeed in their chosen careers.

Discrimination and sexual harassment at work

Women with ASD are at risk for internalizing the underlying assumptions inherent in acts of discrimination. (Gabriels and van Bourgondien 2007, p.xii; Taylor and Seltzer 2010). In this section, Sharon Cowhey and Deborah Thorsos reveal how they have been indoctrinated into thinking women with disabilities, primarily autism, were less valuable as employees and more vulnerable to be victimized by predatory sexual behavior.

Deborah explains how the attributes associated with autism impinged upon her success on the job. She appears to have internalized the social prejudice that made her unacceptable and unworthy of working with customers directly: "My poor posture, crude gait, and speech impediment apparently made people feel uncomfortable placing me in direct contact with the patrons. I didn't mind since I was content in doing solitary work that allowed me to daydream" (Thorsos 2000, p.198). Although she usually attributes her challenges to the symptoms of autism, she does have moments in which she expresses anger about discrimination and exclusion. Deborah sees parallels between discriminatory practices in the workplace and earlier memories of her school days: "My emotions about discrimination boiled to the surface as I associated the feelings of being devalued at work to the childhood discrimination that also affected my self-esteem" (Thorsos 2000, p.294).

While Deborah often accepts and internalizes criticism of her speech, gait, and body language, she is also aware of systemic biases that undervalue her potential and contributions.

Deborah is not the only woman to notice discrimination in the workplace. Sharon Cowhey's feelings about discrimination and abuse in the workplace are far less ambiguous than Deborah's mixed emotions. Sharon places the blame squarely on the shoulders of an oppressive system that breeds exploitation of employees with disabilities:

> The working environment is another difficult place to be. You have to watch out for predators. Supervisors can take major advantage of workers with disabilities. I know, I was one of them. (Cowhey 2005, p.158)

Sharon learned to fear authority figures after suffering several episodes of abuse in the workplace. The negative encounters she had with nondisabled male supervisors and coworkers resulted in a general distrust for authority figures: "Trusting is hard enough, but when you cannot trust certain people in authority, for instance police officers, supervisors, or maybe an ex-husband, or a vindictive friend" (Cowhey 2005, p.66).

After Sharon was sexually harassed by a supervisor at work and her ex-husband was charged with molesting her daughter, she became increasingly apprehensive of nondisabled men in positions of authority. The sexual harassment Sharon suffered at work was incredibly painful, but her eventual diagnosis was an unexpected consequence that occurred when she sought out crisis counseling for employees at her workplace.

Although Sharon started seeing a counselor due to the sexual harassment experienced at work, it was this mental health professional who recognized and finally diagnosed Sharon with autism. With the support of her counselor, Sadie, and family, Sharon gathered the strength to leave her job and sue for damages. "She wanted me to contact a lawyer. Barry agreed, so I contacted a lawyer who handles sexual harassment cases, her name was Mary. With the help of Mary I was finally free! I quit my job and sued them" (Cowhey 2005, p.41). Clearly the sexual abuse Sharon suffered at work was devastating, but finding out about her autism was a key step toward self-acceptance and understanding. Perhaps Sharon resisted the impulse to blame herself for the discrimination and abuse in the workplace because she was not aware that she had autism.

Whereas Deborah had been diagnosed with autism in early childhood and was always aware of her autistic traits, Sharon did not realize some of her attributes and difficulties came from having autism. Deborah appears to have internalized the negative messages she received about autism because she had been indoctrinated into this way of perceiving autism from such an early age. She had had more time to absorb the logic that autism rendered her actions and behavior as inappropriate, undesirable, and deserving to be hidden from view. Sharon avoided this early indoctrination that had taught Deborah to constantly survey herself for the traits of autism and subsequently blame herself for the discrimination she encountered.

Unemployment

Unemployment and underemployment are major issues for women with ASD (Gabriels and van Bourgondien 2007, p.xii; Taylor and Seltzer 2010). Sharon Cowhey, Therese Ronan, and Deborah Thorsos struggled to find satisfying employment that paid a decent wage or provided health benefits. After years of sporadic, poorly paid employment, Sharon found work at a factory that paid an adequate wage. However, she became discouraged and disillusioned by the sexual harassment and general abuse she suffered at work, so she eventually quit and applied for Social Security Disability Insurance. Although Therese Ronan also resisted the harassment and subjugation she endured working at a restaurant by quitting and then using her unemployment benefits to reorganize and find better work, she interpreted unemployment as a personal assessment of her worth and worried about the social meaning of accepting food stamps.

Sharon eventually decided that she did not belong in the workforce, partially due to the stress caused by trying to fit in. The anxiety of her childhood years in school continued into Sharon's working life:

> The few jobs that I worked through the years were usually low paying. But in the time I was married to Greg I worked at a factory, and making what was to me a decent salary. In my world I was quiet and odd, but out in the real world I was a fruitcake! All the years of watching and studying what the normal people were about, I created my own piece of normality. In the eyes of my coworkers they thought of me as the crazy lady, bag lady, or a drug user. By the end of the day I was exhausted. Not only from working, but portraying something I'm not, NORMAL! Just like in

my school days, I couldn't wait to go home and rock.
(Cowhey 2005, p.29)

Sharon noticed a parallel between the pressures of school and
later, employment. When she was employed, she was neither
satisfied with her work, nor was she successful in her efforts to fit
in with coworkers and pass as normal. Sharon responded to
the stress at work just as she had during her school years: she
attempted to escape from her anxiety by spending hours in her
rocking chair.

Deborah Thorsos was unemployed for an extended period
of time while unsuccessfully looking for work. Like Therese,
Deborah took this difficulty quite personally and blamed
herself and her disability when she could not find work:

> I was hurt that I wasn't picked for employment.
> Perhaps I wasn't good enough to be hired even
> at a food service establishment. This confirmed
> my feelings of inferiority. I had difficulty making a
> favorable impression on prospective employers who
> didn't know me or understand my challenges with
> autism. (Thorsos 2000, p.125)

This is yet another instance in which Deborah seems to
have internalized the negative messages she received about
employees with disabilities. She rarely criticized the social
or environmental barriers that kept her from equal access
to employment, just as she shied away from criticizing other
social institutions like school.

Therese, on the other hand, refused to tolerate the harassment
and exploitation she suffered at work:

> I finally quit my job at that restaurant, and I haven't
> regretted it for a minute. The harassment that I
> received while I was working there got to be more

than I could mentally handle. They probably don't miss me either. However, I was in contact with a few other employees. I also have received unemployment compensation. I used that money to purchase stamps and other things that I need to place me back on track. (Ronan 2003, p.128)

Unlike Deborah, who felt pressured to take any job to avoid dependence on her family or public assistance, Therese quit her unsatisfying job and utilized food stamps while finding a more rewarding path.

Sharon Cowhey echoes Therese's disenfranchisement with discriminatory employment practices. After years of underpaid labor, sporadic employment, and unsatisfying jobs, Sharon's employment history ended when her negative experiences culminated in sexual harassment by a coworker: "Barry works very hard to pay the bills, I am on disability. I applied for Social Security Disability after I left my last job. The experience from my last employment was so devastating that it created a great fear in me" (Cowhey 2005, p.43).

Sharon reached a threshold when she could no longer cope with inhospitable work environments, hostile coworkers, or predatory supervisors. Somewhat ironically, her final job turned into an avenue toward diagnosis because it was the workplace crisis counselor who finally recognized the symptoms of autism. Unfortunately, it took a case of sexual harassment to ultimately reveal Sharon's ASD to a professional. She figured that she had suffered at the hands of abusive employers and coworkers long enough to justify her use of public assistance.

While Sharon felt entitled to public assistance, Deborah easily qualified for food stamps based on her need and disability status; however, she was uncomfortable accepting public assistance because of its negative connotation of financial dependence. It is clear that Deborah absorbed the cultural value placed on economic independence: "Though I appreciated getting the food coupons to cover my food costs, I wanted to be hired somewhere with adequate pay and health care benefits" (Thorsos 2000, p.165). Deborah wanted to work and earn a living; she did not want to rely on the government or her family to meet her daily needs. As an educated woman, she believed she should be able to find a decent job; however, employers were not motivated to hire workers with developmental disabilities at that time.

Since the passage of the ADA in 1990, employers are prohibited from discriminatory hiring practices that exclude Americans with disabilities, but there is a growing body of evidence that suggests many highly educated people with autism are still unemployed. Sharon Cowhey, Therese Ronan, and Deborah Thorsos all expressed frustration and self-doubt when unsuccessfully looking for work. When they were fortunate enough to gain employment, the jobs usually consisted of low-paying menial labor that was neither personally fulfilling nor financially adequate.

This chapter has illustrated some of the complex variables that contribute to the success or difficulty the women in this study had in their journey from childhood to adulthood. Temple Grandin achieved her success through a combination of personal talent and social support, but had the benefit of a supportive family, talented mentors, and personal initiative. Erika Hammerschmidt and Deborah Thorsos had supportive families, but were not able to apply their college education or natural talents toward a meaningful career. Sharon Cowhey did not have the support of her family, a high school diploma, or supportive employers and ultimately resigned from the workforce to collect Social Security. Therese

Ronan was in conflict with her family and was not permitted to train for a career in the beauty industry, but resisted the pressure to conform to a marginal or subservient status. Dawn Prince-Hughes had supportive parents, but struggled through her childhood, adolescence, and into adulthood. She had to contend with the social stigma of being openly gay and missing an autism diagnosis, but ultimately achieved her educational and professional goals. Liane Holliday Willey anticipated having a successful career, just as she had with her college education, but without an awareness of autism, she struggled to understand the issues that led to her difficulty and anxiety.

CHAPTER FOUR

SEXUAL DEVELOPMENT AND ROMANTIC RELATIONSHIPS

In this chapter I examine some of the themes that emerged in the lives of these women as they transitioned throughout the physiological changes brought on by puberty. The first section reveals a unique issue for girls with developmental disabilities like ASD. Second, the women discuss the ways in which they had difficulties understanding the unwritten rules of romance. The third section reveals how disability identity played an integral role in the women's search for a partnership and marriage. The fourth stresses the importance of past relationships and crushes that were helpful learning experiences. In the last section I show how families and communities influence sexual development.

Disparities between sexual and emotional development

Girls with ASD are often aware of the changes taking place during puberty, but sometimes feel a disparity between their emotional development and chronological age (Gabriels and van Bourgondien 2007; Tissot 2009). Deborah Thorsos and Sharon Cowhey were aware of the physical and hormonal changes occurring during puberty, regardless of any developmental delay or the social and communicative impairments associated with autism. They describe a gap between physical maturation and emotional development that shaped a feeling of discomfort with the overall process of puberty.

Deborah explains how early physical maturity stood in contrast to her emotional immaturity. This distance between physical development and psychological maturity was exacerbated for Deborah, who had begun puberty earlier than other girls her age:

> A few months before my tenth birthday as I was about to enter puberty, my hormonal level started to act up and affect me. I became more moody, irritable, and depressed. I began to develop physically at a very young age while I was still emotionally immature. (Thorsos 2000, p.45)

Deborah describes how psychological and emotional delays seemed more pronounced by her early entrance into puberty. The physical changes occurring during puberty became more challenging for her because she felt unprepared to deal with the social and emotional changes. For example, she did not feel emotionally ready to handle the hygienic responsibilities that came with menstruation.

When Sharon reached adolescence, she was acutely aware that her "interest in boys started becoming stronger" (Cowhey 2005, p.19). Like Deborah, Sharon reported a lapse between physical and emotional development that became particularly problematic during adolescence. Although she was aware of her sexual development, she did not feel emotionally equipped to handle the responsibility of becoming sexually active: "I knew nothing about having a relationship with a boy, I knew nothing about what to do in any kind of life's situations, and all I knew was how to rock with music blasting in my ears to escape into my world" (Cowhey 2005, p.20).

Sharon yearned to escape from her life as an adolescent girl with undiagnosed autism. Throughout her life she coped with anxiety by rocking for hours in a rocking chair. This may have prefaced a general need to escape from stress and anxiety rather than managing negative feelings in a more productive way. The need for escape was clearly demonstrated in childhood, which is when her addiction to rocking began. Before adolescence, Sharon's methods of escape were limited to emotional acts, that is, forgetting her worries in the motion of the chair and accompanying music. During adolescence, she had greater opportunities and more freedom to physically remove herself from stressful situations. After becoming sexually mature, Sharon was able to physically escape from the anxiety of her daily life by running away from home with a boyfriend. However, many of the same issues that troubled her at school followed her after she left, and became problematic in this romantic relationship. As this relationship ended, Sharon became involved with another young man who had a criminal record. Once again, her social, sensory, and communication difficulties threatened her desire to have a healthy mature relationship: "My relationship with Jeter was coming to an end.

After all, at that time I didn't even know the definition of the word relationship. If he asked to have sex, I would" (Cowhey 2005, p.21).

Sharon's underdeveloped comprehension of the fundamental principles of sexuality or lack of sociosexual knowledge has been demonstrated in the existing research on autism and sexuality. Lack of sociosexual knowledge is the first of these factors. Sociosexual knowledge plateaus around the age of puberty; individuals with AS at that age have rarely attained the maturity of the average young adult. They do not have the same experiences as adolescents in the general population (Griffith *et al.* 1999; Henault 2006; Hingsburger *et al.* 1993; Kelly *et al.* 2008; Realmuto and Ruble 1999). Deborah and Sharon recognized that their bodies and feelings were changing, but did not always feel prepared for the challenges that came with sexual development. Deborah, born in 1957, and Sharon, born in 1959, were contemporaries; however, Deborah had been diagnosed in early childhood and received ongoing outside support whereas Sharon was not diagnosed until adulthood and struggled to understand the reason behind her social awkwardness and overwhelming anxiety. Nevertheless, both women recognized a disconnect between physical and emotional development that became increasingly obvious during the transitional period of adolescence.

Difficulties understanding the unwritten rules of romance

Women with ASD report feelings of confusion and frustration when trying to comprehend the complicated, unwritten rules of romance and courtship (Gougeon 2010; Mehzabin and Stokes 2011; Tissot 2009). All of the women in this study corroborate this phenomenon. Dawn Prince-Hughes may not have commented on her confusion over romance during adolescence, but she definitely reported these issues in adulthood. She already had to contend with undiagnosed autism, the stigma of being openly gay during a time when it was not socially acceptable, being bullied because of her sexual identity, alcoholism, and dropping out of high school. Confusion over romance would have to wait until adulthood.

Liane Holliday Willey was aware that her typically developing girlfriends were interacting with boys in new ways, but flirtatious behavior was difficult to interpret and harder to emulate. She remembered this period as a pivotal departure from mainstream social development:

> They were giggling and laughing and tossing their hair behind their shoulders, gently putting their hands on the boys' arms, looking totally lost in the limelight of the attention they were getting. I could see their formula but I could not bring myself to follow it... Only then did I realize that I had been tossed aside... I never understood their vernacular. Suffice to say that, at that point, I was unable to read between the lines. Subtext and innuendo may as well have been birds flying by my window. (Holliday Willey 1999, pp.45–46)

In this excerpt, Liane maintains that she understood flirtation on a very basic level, but the deeper subtext eluded her. She was aware that her peers were interacting in new and different ways; further, she had some insight into how these shifting conventions of behavior worked. However, she had trouble understanding the more subtle cues presented by flirtation, and also how to implement these new modes of conversation and behavior.

Liane may have felt she had some insight into romance during adolescence, albeit limited. By the time she reached adulthood, she had formed serious doubts about her ability to communicate well enough to initiate or maintain a romantic relationship. Her romantic experiences during adolescence and early adulthood contributed to deeper reservations about her ability to effectively communicate with another person well enough to have a romantic relationship:

> By the time I met my husband I was pretty well convinced I would never understand anyone well enough to maintain something everlasting... My AS behaviors—the sensory integration problems, literal mindedness, perseverance and rigid thinking tendencies—acted like arrows tipped in poison that stood poised and ready to pierce every relationship I ever found... From the moment I met Tom, I sensed he was a great deal like me. (Holliday Willey 1999, p.62)

Based on her adolescent experiences, Liane doubted her ability to understand and interpret the verbal and nonverbal forms of communication well enough to satisfy a romantic partner. The fact that she had not been diagnosed with autism during her development appears to have exacerbated the confusion she felt when trying to understand why she had so much difficulty with interpersonal relationships. Liane's doubts about finding an intimate partner were fueled by her confusion in romantic scenarios, and also because she did not know that autism was the reason behind her confusion. Although she was undiagnosed during adolescence, the communication impairments associated with autism were still problematic for her.

Sharon Cowhey, like Liane Holliday Willey, was not diagnosed with autism until she reached adulthood. Likewise, Sharon reiterated Liane's narrative about the struggle to find romance given the social and communication impairments of autism. Sharon saw autism as a hindrance to her sexuality because the symptoms of autism made it difficult to interpret the social norms governing courtship and attraction: "Autism has prevented me from being sexy and romantic so having sex for the first time was for me a very painful unwanted pleasure" (Cowhey 2005, p.21).

Sharon, like Liane, was frustrated by her difficulty understanding and interpreting sexual behavior. She wanted to feel sexy and romantic but, like Liane, did not have an autism diagnosis that would help to explain why this was so challenging. Sharon's lack of healthy sexual life skills resulted in more than frustration. Sharon had a child as an unwed teenage mother. Her first marriage ended because her partner was sexually abusing her daughter. She also became a victim of sexual harassment at work. Although she expresses some satisfaction in her current marriage, Sharon's husband abuses alcohol, which causes problems in their relationship.

Although Erika Hammerschmidt was diagnosed with autism in early childhood, she still wrestled with the same type of frustration with romance that distressed Liane and Sharon. Unlike Liane and Sharon, she knew why she had difficulties with style and socialization, but this awareness did little to offset her feelings of alienation and inadequacy:

> I wore tight, low-necked shirts, but didn't know I was supposed to wear anything under them for modesty. I wore lots of makeup—too much, and the wrong colors. I had no idea what went with what. And even when I did manage to look beautiful, it didn't make

up for being a weirdo. I had the same desire for love and popularity that all girls had, but it took me a long time to learn to fulfill it in a healthy way. Throughout my childhood, teens and young adulthood, I struggled to fit in. (Hammerschmidt 2005, p.5)

In adolescence, Erika became increasingly frustrated by the challenges of understanding, interpreting, and implementing standards of personal appearance and interpersonal communication:

I was angry that nobody desired me—that I probably wouldn't ever have any chance of losing my virginity. I didn't know how to dress to attract men, even how to talk to attract them. Angry at myself because, whenever I found a guy attractive, I just came up to him and made a crude joke about wanting to tear off his clothes, and as a result he neither felt comfortable with me nor took my desire seriously. (Hammerschmidt 2005, p.84)

Erika resented the fact that she felt so bewildered by the opposite sex, and seems to have turned this anger inward, blaming herself and her disability for this confusion. Romance and relationships appear to have followed a general rule of feeling alienated from others, a feeling that has permeated every aspect of Erika's life. Just as the title of her autobiography, *Born on the Wrong Planet* (2005), suggests, Erika related to human society as if it was an alien culture. Her alienation was twofold; on one level, she felt alienated, as in set apart or separated from others in an existential way, while on another level, she related to the fictional alien Spock from *Star Trek* because she found human society to be just as foreign as another planet. (Temple Grandin also reported a particular affinity for the character Spock for similar reasons.)

> I had reached a point where I had resigned myself
> to being single, and wasn't sure I could handle a
> romantic relationship anyway. "There are times,"
> I had recently written to Internet friends, "when I fear
> that this 'alien trapped in a human body' feeling goes
> as deep as my sexual orientation, and I am simply
> not attracted to people from this planet." All my
> life I'd had trouble with romance. (Hammerschmidt
> 2005, p.140)

Like Liane, Erika reached a point where she became resigned
to the idea that she might never form a long-term relationship.
Erika looked toward the future with apprehension because she
doubted her ability to attract a romantic partner or exert her
own sexuality successfully. Her transition into adulthood was
filled with self-doubt concerning her ability to date or marry.

Whereas Erika directed her anger inward, Therese Ronan
realized that her romantic opportunities were limited based
on discrimination against people with disabilities. Therese
sees disability as an obstacle in her romantic life. Her history
of negative experiences with love reinforces her tendency to
fantasize about romance rather than experience it firsthand.
Her first love interests were movie stars or teen heart-throbs.
As a teenager, a friend's brother became her "first, non-fantasy-
world crush" (Ronan 2003, p.38). Unfortunately, Therese's
feelings were not shared by many of her crushes, which she
attributes to her disability:

> If you have a mental disability, you may have a crush
> on a guy, but your chances of his liking you as well
> are much less. I got crushes on guys who weren't
> even in my life. I figured if they didn't know me, then
> they couldn't respond to me with hateful emotions.
> So there are several differences that I know for a fact

between those with disabilities and those without.
(Ronan 2003, p.29)

Therese distinguishes herself from the other women in this
book because she was the only one to point to stigma and
discrimination, rather than the communication and skills
associated with autism.

Erika, like Deborah, was diagnosed with autism in childhood.
However, Erika was born in 1981 whereas Deborah was born
in 1957, so Erika attended integrated schools with her peers
while Deborah was segregated in special education from an
early age. Perhaps Deborah absorbed these messages more
easily because she was diagnosed in early childhood and grew
up in an era of widespread educational segregation, based
on race and disability. She may have eventually accepted the
negative messages about autism that were ingrained in systems
of segregation and special education. In the following example,
Deborah provides a textbook account of her social deficits and
how they infringed upon her ability to find a quality companion:
"My deficits in appearance, social skills, and self-confidence,
which were painfully obvious, made it challenging for a man
I would be interested in to make me his girlfriend" (Thorsos
2000, p.211).

Deborah appears to have wholeheartedly internalized the
defining features of autism without much resistance. According
to Dubin (2014, p.59), "Besides what they heard or read in the
media, those on the spectrum have also personally received
negative messages about certain autistic traits over which
they have no control." Deborah responded to the hegemony of
segregation built into the social systems that pervaded her life
from early childhood. After years of early intervention, special
education, and rehabilitative efforts, Deborah saw herself from

a medical perspective that emphasized deficits and impairments over and above the social or political circumstances that limited her opportunities, and seems to have accepted the professional assessment of her impairments without question.

Temple Grandin, a contemporary of Deborah, has disregarded her chances for romance completely and opted for an asexual lifestyle. Temple does not explicitly discuss adolescent events connected to romance or crushes, but one might speculate that the absence of these formative experiences influenced her later decision to avoid intimacy altogether:

> Although business relationships can easily be learned by rote, dating is difficult. The social skills one needs to rent an apartment and keep a job were easier for me to learn than the social skills for dating, because I have very few emotional cues to guide me during complex social interactions. (Grandin 2006, p.155)

Unlike Deborah, who still made efforts to form intimate relationships despite the social impairments that make intimacy challenging for people with autism, Temple completely avoided romance. Although she had learned that she possessed poor communication and social skills, Deborah was still interested in pursuing romantic relationships; despite thinking that it was doubtful, she still made an effort. Temple, on the other hand, appears to have rejected romance outright, also absorbing and transmitting the negative message that romantic relationships were simply too difficult for people with the social and sensory impairments of autism: "I've remained celibate because doing so helps me to avoid the many complicated social situations that are too difficult for me to handle. For most people with autism, physical closeness is as much a problem as not understanding basic social behaviors" (Grandin 2006, p.154).

Except for Temple Grandin, the other women in this book voiced a desire for intimate relationships with a significant other. However, they did not always understand the unwritten rules of romance and courtship. Temple is the only woman in this group to actively choose abstinence. Liane Holliday Willey, Sharon Cowhey, Erika Hammerschmidt, and Deborah Thorsos married, while Dawn Prince-Hughes is in a committed partnership. Therese Ronan wanted to marry, but was thwarted by the efforts of her family who intervened to end the engagement.

The women in this book unanimously agree that ASD poses unique challenges to forming and maintaining romantic relationships. Liane, Sharon, Erika, Deborah, and Temple all pointed to the core impairments of autism that made communication and socialization difficult, especially in potentially romantic scenarios. Dawn experienced the same sort of confusion, but her experiences were limited to adulthood. Therese was the only woman to move beyond blaming the symptoms of autism for restricting her love life and took a more socio-political stance, highlighting stigma and prejudice against people with disabilities.

Disability identity and romance

This section looks at the ways women with ASD connect with romantic interests through the common experience of disability. Special education presented early opportunities to form crushes, flirt, and begin dating. Erika Hammerschmidt had several young loves during childhood and early adolescence followed by a frustrating drought, with very few romantic prospects. In college, she met her future husband through a network of friends and acquaintances on the autism spectrum.

Deborah Thorsos also dated several people on the autism spectrum, but found that they were incompatible. Ultimately, having a disability identity brought her into contact with her future husband, a man who is visually impaired and also relies on public transport.

One of Erika's young relationships developed at a summer camp for children in special education:

> In junior high school I spent part of one summer in a special ed. summer program, where the students did things like going to parks, swimming pools, and libraries and so on. One of the guys said quite bluntly to me one day at the pool that he wanted to be my boyfriend. Having no other romantic prospects in sight, I agreed. We never kissed, but we sat together on the bus every day with our arms around each other. (Hammerschmidt 2005, p.77)

Having a disability community was crucial for Erika's first introduction to romance and dating, and later became an integral support system that led to her meeting her husband:

> We exchanged several emails and phone calls before arranging a date. He talked about how struck he was by my cleverness at the party, and later by my website and an article he had read about my book. He had ordered the book online and looked forward to reading it. He never said outright that he was in love or had a crush on me, but it glared out from between the lines. (Hammerschmidt 2005, p.142)

After years of frustration searching for love, Erika found companionship with a man who is also on the autism spectrum. They eventually married and adopted a parrot, but do not plan to have children. From her first childhood experience of puppy love at that special ed. camp, to eventually finding her mate at an Aspire party, Erika had more success dating in the disability community.

Deborah found her first boyfriend at school; he also had some language irregularities due to mild autism. At that point in time, Deborah found it difficult to tolerate his intense speaking style due to her own sensory issues:

> In school there was one boy, Stuart, in my class and van who was attracted to me. He was like my first boyfriend. He sat next to me as much is possible. We liked each other very much and we gave each other cards for birthdays and holidays, including Valentine's Day. He was very intelligent and had mild autism. He, like me, talked too much and loudly. However unlike me, he talked on and on with excessive details on technical matters. This made it more difficult for me to listen. (Thorsos 2000, p.35)

Although this relationship was short-lived, Deborah had this early opportunity to practice some of the customs of courtship. Her relationship with Stuart may have set the stage for future intimate relationships based on a shared disability identity:

> This was my very first real date. The main problem was that he talked non-stop and I had difficulty listening to him. I was unable to process the onslaught of all that auditory information due to my sensory overload and attention problems. He must have picked up that I wasn't taking in everything he said to me though I tried very hard to listen the effect became a strain on me after just a few minutes of his monologue. The strain was compounded by my not having much to say myself. At the end of our only date, as I was getting ready to go home, he decided

> to break up with me. I didn't blame him and I wasn't
> hurt. I realized he wanted someone to act as a
> sounding board which was beyond me; anyway the
> breakup was a relief to me. I wasn't ready to sustain
> an intimate relationship such as having a boyfriend.
> Carrying on conversations wasn't one of my fortes,
> one of the major qualities that enhance intimacy.
> (Thorsos 2000, p.93)

Her first date with Stuart was complicated by the fact that
they both had autism. In that instance, the nuances of their
disabilities caused them to clash with each other. Stuart ended
the relationship at the end of that first date, but the overall
experience was constructive for Deborah because it gave her
an example of a type of relationship that would not work.

A shared experience of disability is a defining feature of
the relationship between Deborah and her husband, Chris.
Although Chris is visually impaired while Deborah has autism,
they each recognize disability as a shared identity that unites
their relationship:

> After Chris and I talked to each other about our past
> and the challenges we endured, we were drawn to
> each other by a mutual understanding of having
> a disability and dealing with it, even though our
> problems were very different. It was love at first sight,
> there was a mutual attraction and both of us felt that
> we were right for each other. Chris was impressed
> with my college education and intelligence and,
> likewise, I was impressed with his. He was also close
> to my age being only 3½ years older than me. (Thorsos
> 2000, p.217)

At this point in her life, Deborah was ready for intimacy and had
the experience to realize what she truly wanted in a partner.

She may not have had the skills or opportunity to form an intimate relationship in the past, but it seems that practice improved her confidence and deepened her understanding of intimacy.

Special education provided Erika and Deborah with a peer group united by disability, which was instrumental to forming their first romantic relationships. These early relationships, shaped by a common experience of disability, may have set the stage for future partnerships built on a shared sense of disability identity.

The importance of practice

Children and adolescents with ASD need opportunities to learn and practice social skills, but may not have the same chances to socialize with nondisabled peers (DeMatteo *et al.* 2012). Erika Hammerschmidt and Deborah Thorsos highlight how romantic relationships are built upon social skills that require practice and opportunity.

Erika remembers meeting one of her first boyfriends at a language immersion summer camp. Having an interest in common with her typically developing peers at camp enabled her to thrive socially:

> We kissed in public, so addicted to the new feeling that we didn't care what other people thought. We kissed in the nurse's office when I was sick for a few days and he was allowed in to see me. We kissed once when I was wearing my retainer. (Hammerschmidt 2005, p.122)

Erika's relationship with Pablo coincided with general acceptance at camp that summer, reinforcing the idea that practicing social skills bolsters romantic relationships. She had two more love interests during junior high school that allowed her to exercise some of these emerging skills. However, the development of her romantic social skills was put on hold when romantic options dwindled in high school:

> Those three situations were the closest I got to romance for many years. Each one took up only a few weeks of my childhood, with long lonely months and years in between. Looking back, it's hard even to think of them as boyfriends, but as I went through high school without a love interest, I wished I hadn't gotten tired of them so fast. (Hammerschmidt 2005, p.78)

Erika was frustrated by the romantic lull she faced in high school, and wished she had savored those earlier relationships. She had at least had a rudimentary introduction to romantic relationships, although she would have preferred more options.

Deborah also highlights how crucial it is to practice daily social interactions. She credits the structure and predictability of regular employment for providing her with an environment to build her social skills: "As I intersected with many kinds of people day to day at work, I experienced a growth in social skills that enabled me to form intimate relationships with a close friend and even a steady boyfriend" (Thorsos 2000, p.224). Deborah demonstrates how exposure to other people on a regular basis improved her confidence and ability to form deeper, more intimate relationships. As she looks back on past experiences, she recognizes her mistakes and now takes steps towards better communication and social skills.

This section reveals a potentially political issue tied up in this need for practice, that is, many adults with autism are underserved by social services and often become unemployed. Without typical peer groups, knowledge of social skills, or opportunities for employment, adults with autism have very few outlets to develop and utilize social skills. Without these vital social skills, many adults with autism are again limited in their chances for romance.

The role of family and community

Families and communities can influence the romantic development of girls and women with ASD (Kelly *et al.* 2008; van Pelt 2008). The families of Therese Ronan and Dawn Prince-Hughes impacted their romantic lives in very different ways. For Therese, family played a detrimental role when they intervened to end her engagement. After finding someone who returned her affections, Therese's family ended the relationship with the help of law enforcement:

> I dated a young man named Tom for a while and was engaged to him for two days. I had met him at a mental health meeting. He was a tall, thin brunette. One night we went to a motel in a nearby town. We planned to run away and get married the next day. In the morning after breakfast, he decided to take me ring shopping. We took a cab to the shopping center. To our surprise, when we arrived, the police, my dad, and Tom's mom were there. We had to go home. That was the end of our friendship. I don't know how they knew where we were. I saw Tom another time after that. Then we broke up. (Ronan 2003, p.63)

Therese's family demonstrated their discomfort with her sexuality and their apparent authority to control her love life. Historically, the reproductive health and sexuality of people with disabilities has been ignored, denied, oppressed, or controlled by family members, medical professionals, and social ideologies. Most notably, many people with disabilities were involuntarily sterilized during the height of the Eugenics movement (Block 2000; Snyder and Mitchell 2002, 2010).

On the other hand, Dawn Prince-Hughes benefited from parents who supported her during the process of discovering her sexual orientation:

> As I told them about my feelings, my parents listened carefully and did not make much comment. Soon afterward my mother started driving me down to the nearest city of any size (an hour away) so that I could explore a group run by gay and lesbian people. I had no interest in dating for sexual reasons and still felt that sexuality ran on a continuum. (Prince-Hughes 2004, p.58)

The members of her gay support group were compassionate and sincere, although they did not always understand her. Although Dawn did not receive an autism diagnosis until she was fully grown, her family's support during adolescence allowed her to claim a sexual identity without knowing she had autism. Several conclusions could be drawn from this example, such that family support might outweigh the importance of having a diagnosis during the transition to adulthood.

The group was also crucial to addressing her alcoholic behavior during adolescence: "I think the other people involved cared about me and wanted to be supportive, even if at times they didn't understand me. I know they worried about my drinking as well" (Prince-Hughes 2004, p.59).

The support group provided Dawn with a safe space without knowing she had autism. This supportive community may have enabled Dawn to come to terms with her sexuality and deal with alcoholism long before she was diagnosed with autism. The Prince family played a positive role in smoothing Dawn's transition to adulthood by accepting and supporting their daughter's sexuality.

In sharp contrast, Therese Ronan and Dawn Prince-Hughes demonstrate how family attitudes influence the sexuality and romantic prospects of girls with ASD. Therese's family refused to recognize her as an adult woman who could make her own decisions. On the other hand, the Prince family rallied to help Dawn form a healthy sexual identity.

This chapter has showcased five themes that the women in this study encountered during their transition from childhood to womanhood. Sharon Cowhey and Deborah Thorsos address disparities between sexual and emotional developments. Then Sharon, Deborah, Erika, Liane, Therese, and Temple discuss the difficulties in understanding the unwritten rules of romance. In the section on disability identity and romance, Erika and Deborah reveal how a shared experience of disability added to their loneliness. Deborah and Erika then stress how opportunities to learn and practice emerging social skills are crucial to forming romantic relationships. Finally, Therese and Dawn expose the powerful influence that families and communities exert on girls with ASD becoming women.

CHAPTER FIVE

FAMILY, FRIENDS, AND OTHER NETWORKS OF SUPPORT

This chapter considers the importance of family, religion, friendship, and systems of socialization in the lives of women with ASD. These social systems play integral roles in the development of girls with ASD on their path toward adulthood. In reflecting on this process the women reveal how communities based on family, faith, and friendships helped or hindered their transition from girlhood to womanhood. The first section features the instrumental role played by supportive families. The second describes how the lack of information about autism compounds family stress. The third examines the ramifications of passing ASD from one generation to the next. The fourth describes the family dynamics that influence self-image. The fifth outlines how parents can steer girls with ASD toward support groups and other organizations. In the sixth section we learn how girls and women with ASD benefit from inclusion into the spiritual life of the family. Conversely, the seventh section illustrates what happens when girls and women with ASD are excluded from the religious practices of their family. The eighth section highlights a major issue for girls and women with ASD, which is the struggle to make lasting friendships. Ending on a positive note, the final section emphasizes examples of girls and women with ASD forming meaningful friendships.

Supportive families

The support of family is critical to the success of women with ASD during school and beyond (Hartmann 2012; Plumb 2011). Temple Grandin and Deborah Thorsos successfully received their high school diplomas during a time in American history before laws like the IDEA and ADA were passed to ensure the civil rights of people with disabilities. Staying in school was a major accomplishment at a time when others, such as Therese Ronan, missed two years of school. Erika Hammerschmidt reinforces the importance of supportive parents to provide a supportive and loving home life in which she was able to pursue her creative interests and express her personality.

Temple Grandin stresses the importance of the type of individual attention her mother gave her on a daily basis. Given the period in which Temple was born and raised, keeping her in school and out of an institution was no easy task:

> My mother spent thirty minutes five days a week for several months teaching me to read… Mother had a knack for recognizing which people could help me and which ones could not. She sought out the best teachers and schools for me, in an era when most autistic children were placed in institutions. She was determined to keep me out of an institution. (Grandin 2006, p.46)

Temple realizes that it was not only her mother, but also a network of caregivers and professionals that supported her education and success: "I am lucky in that I responded well when my mother, teachers, and governess kept encouraging social interaction and play. I was seldom allowed to retreat into the soothing world of rocking or spinning objects. When I daydreamed, my teachers yanked me back to reality" (Grandin 2006, p.43).

This demonstrates the need for a strong network of support, and also Temple's perspective on self-stimulation or stims that often accompany an ASD diagnosis. In fact, the presence of repetitive, stereotyped movements are still a defining feature of an ASD diagnosis, according to the DSM-5 (APA 2013, p.50). However, not all people with ASD share this viewpoint.

Erika Hammerschmidt's parents enabled her to better understand her environment and find a comfortable way to connect with it. Her parents supported her creative endeavors, which aided her to comprehend and envision a future that held a place for her:

> Mom and Dad have always supported me in my struggle to come to terms with my Asperger Syndrome, and perhaps they sensed that writing and other forms of artwork play a large role in this struggle. I have learned to understand the rest of the world by writing about it, and when I have been unable to understand it, I have taken refuge in other worlds I've created through writing, painting and drawing. I cannot remember a time when my creative urges were not met. (Hammerschmidt 2005, p.27)

The support of her parents at an early age enabled her to face adulthood with a hopeful and positive attitude. Whereas Temple credits her parents for keeping her engaged in reality,

Erika is thankful that her parents allowed her the freedom to retreat into her own world. This turned out to be beneficial for Erika because it was in that imaginary space where she gained a greater understanding of her own culture. Throughout her autobiography, Erika explains how her imagination and writing served as a parallel to human culture, and eventually became a metaphorical bridge to actual human civilization.

Deborah Thorsos recognizes her dependence on her family beginning in girlhood, but this knowledge guided her towards positive choices that supported her future development: "Since I didn't have a strong social network outside my immediate family due to my autism, it was even more vital that I continue to live where I could receive the support of my family" (Thorsos 2000, p.94). The support of her family was a compelling factor behind Deborah's successful transition into adulthood. Deborah benefited from having a supportive family, but also the personal realization that being in close proximity to her family was critical to her development.

Therese Ronan remembers her family being generally supportive, but also relates how her family underestimated her intelligence and treated her in an unequal way. She portrays a more complex relationship between herself and family members; although she feels they have been supportive, she also feels belittled by their low assessment of her intelligence:

> It was nice that they remembered me with all the hassle that I put them through. All of my brothers and their wives came to the party. It's times like these that I really am grateful for such a wonderful family. Whether I'm autistic or disabled, they have been real good to me for the most part of my life. Nevertheless, I also feel that I was treated as if I were without a brain. But they have stood by me through thick and thin. (Ronan 2003, p.122)

Looking back, Therese appreciated the general support of her family, but presents her family history as a mixed bag of emotions and experiences. Had her family been more positive in her youth, she may have had a better opinion of her status in the family.

Erika, Temple, and Deborah consistently present positive images of their families and the beneficial role they played in their lives. Therese, on the other hand, remembers a more complex relationship with her family who often relegated her to a secondary place.

Lack of information adds to family stress

Coming of age during the era immediately following the identification of autism as a diagnostic term in 1943 brought particular challenges for baby boomer women with ASD (Baron-Cohen 1997; Hacking 2009). Temple Grandin was born only four years after Kanner introduced the term "autism" as a diagnostic label. Prior to Kanner, Bleuler used the term autism to describe a type of schizophrenia (Bleuler 2010; Clifford et al. 2007; Davidson 2007; Stanghellini 2001).

In an era when little was known about autism, Temple Grandin's parents pursued a diagnosis when she failed to reach early developmental benchmarks: "Mother first realized that something was drastically wrong when I failed to start talking like the little girl next door, and it seemed that I might be deaf" (Grandin 2006, p.33). In Temple's situation, the strength of her parents' conviction led to a diagnosis that was not as widely publicized or well known as it is today. This led Temple's mother to employ extraordinary means to communicate with her daughter, which may have primed Temple for future success with interpersonal communication.

Deborah Thorsos, born ten years after Temple, still grappled with the limitations of having an ASD diagnosis at that particular time:

> The challenges of caring for a person with a disability, especially when very little was known about it, tended to affect the dynamics of the entire family including me. It was emotionally draining for my entire family, especially when I exhibited enigmatic behaviors and was unable to communicate. (Thorsos 2000, p.20)

Deborah explores how public knowledge about autism, or lack of it, influenced the ways her family dealt with her disability. The family's perspective on her disability was informed by a lack of information about autism at that time, and this was an ongoing issue.

Temple and Deborah outline the central roles that parents and families played in their lives. Although imperfect, these women report that their families provided communities that supported their transition from girls with autism to women with autism.

Genealogies of neurodivergence

Research suggests that ASD is genetically transmitted from one generation to the next (APA 2013; Hu-Lince *et al.* 2005; Jamain *et al.* 2003; Muhle, Trentacoste, and Rapin 2004). In an emerging phenomenon, many adults receive an ASD diagnosis after their child or close relative receives a similar diagnosis.

For example, Liane Holliday Willey began to identify with ASD after her daughter was formally diagnosed. In a similar fashion, those diagnosed with ASD look to past generations for evidence of autism in their parents and other family members. Deborah Thorsos and Sharon Cowhey identify their fathers as the genetic source for their own autism. Neither father was formally diagnosed with autism, but they had certain characteristic traits consistent with autism. Deborah listed her father's autistic-like behaviors:

> My father had some autistic characteristics although he was never diagnosed as a child. He displayed autistic behaviors: nose picking in public, poor table manners, compulsive behaviors, imbalanced emotions, and social ineptitude. (Thorsos 2000, p.16)

Deborah felt her father's affection in spite of his difficulties that she attributes to autism: "Beneath his disability, I felt his love of the family including me. He had difficulty raising us children. But, it was basically my mother raised us since she did not have autism" (Thorsos 2000, p.17).

The parenting responsibilities fell mainly on the shoulders of Deborah's mother because her father did not have the capacity to emotionally support his children. This may have taxed the relationship between her parents because they eventually divorced. However, had he been diagnosed, Mr Thorsos could have provided a different and unique type of social support that could have been instructive to Deborah while making that transition into adulthood.

Sharon, like Deborah, also points to her father as the genetic source of her autism. Unlike Deborah, Sharon did not feel loved or nurtured by her father regardless of his disability. Rather, Sharon's father was aloof and addicted to alcohol:

My father never showed much affection towards
anyone. As I look back at the way my father was,
I feel my autism came from him. My father was an
alcoholic. I understood him because I felt he could
not stop drinking just like I could not stop rocking.
(Cowhey 2005, p.23)

Whereas Mr Thorsos raises the potential for a parent with
autism becoming especially supportive to a daughter with autism, Mr Cowhey demonstrates how a parent's undiagnosed
autism could add chaos to family life. In Sharon's case, her
father's lack of affection and dependence on alcohol may have
negatively impacted Sharon throughout her developmental
process. Mr Cowhey's alcoholism appears to have led to
Sharon's affinity toward her current husband, another
alcoholic. In fact, Sharon sees parallels between the destructive
behaviors exemplified by both her father and husband: "My
father being an alcoholic drove drunk. Every time he would
do this it worried me. Barry drinks and when he drinks and
drives he worries me too" (Cowhey 2005, p.61). This suggests
that feelings she first associated with her father's drinking
resurfaced in connection to her husband's drinking. At the very
least, this suggests that Sharon was familiar, if not comfortable,
with alcoholic behaviors.

Although Sharon and Deborah both believe their fathers
had many autistic characteristics and may have simply had
cases of undiagnosed autism, that is where the similarity ends.
Deborah felt loved and valued by her father, regardless of his
own condition. Unlike Deborah, Sharon did not feel nurtured
by her father, but autism wasn't the only source of difficulty;
alcoholism emotionally affected her psyche and may have
prepared her for a future marriage with another alcoholic.

Family shapes attitudes about disability

The way one's family understands autism can influence the way girls and women perceive their own disability (Baron-Cohen 1997; Hacking 2009; Hartmann 2012; Plumb 2011). Dawn Prince-Hughes, Deborah Thorsos, and Sharon Cowhey describe the ways in which family shaped their attitudes about themselves.

Dawn has a particularly tender memory of her father attempting to comfort her during hard times at the beginning of adolescence. She remembers "he was trying hard to help me but had to admit that he and my mother had considered finding a hospital for me" (Prince-Hughes 2004, p.51). Her parents' fears reinforced her own anxiety about her potential to care for herself in the future:

> My parents tried to come to check on me as best they could and bring me things to make my life easier, but I was losing contact with them, moving away from them and into nothingness. I was ashamed that I couldn't function, and sometimes I avoided them when I knew they were coming. (Prince-Hughes 2004, p.64)

Her inability to care for herself was a source of insecurity for her, and it seems her parents' low assessment of her life skills reinforced this attitude. Dawn's parents were concerned about her when she was still a child, but without a diagnosis, Dawn's issues must have seemed mysterious and unusual. Her parents' early concern for her future enhanced her own doubts about her ability to care for herself as an adult.

Deborah worried about her future in terms of becoming a financial burden to her family:

> Without a job or any government funds I wouldn't be able to afford rent on my own. I didn't want to depend on my parents for rent money or want my mother and Tom or Bob and Jen to be forced to take me into their homes and become a burden to them if I couldn't make money. (Thorsos 2000, p.186)

Deborah was driven to find a job and earn money, rather than exploring her interests. In this case, she was afraid that her family would perceive her in a negative light if she could not contribute financially. She found work in a cafeteria, even though she was overeducated for that position. The fear of becoming a burden to her family appears to have played a significant role in her transition to adulthood.

Sharon Cowhey also sees autism in ways that are informed by her family's needs and opinions:

> I am sure my family has been affected by me in more ways than one. But because I cannot go back in life, I do have some regrets, especially on how I did not hug my mother or comfort my sister Angel's two children when they were little. If I could be just a little normal I would have been a better daughter to my parents. (Cowhey 2005, p.94)

Sharon's regrets demonstrate the connection between autism and the social conventions that govern family relationships and responsibilities. In this way, she reveals how her self-image is informed by the role autism plays within the context of the family unit. Autism does not exist in a vacuum; in other words, it becomes a limitation when the social environment conflicts with the neurology of individuals with autism.

Dawn, Deborah, and Sharon consider how family attitudes influenced the ways they viewed themselves throughout the process of development—Dawn's parents exacerbated her own concerns about her ability to survive as an adult, Deborah's concern about becoming a burden to her family led her to take a job far beneath her education, and Sharon's family bolstered the idea that her disability was an obstacle to her fulfilling traditional family roles and obligations.

Families connect girls with ASD to support systems

Family plays an integral role in the developmental process of women with ASD in direct ways and also as a catalyst for connecting to more formal networks of support (Meadan, Halle, and Ebata 2010; Renty and Roeyers 2006b). This was true for Deborah Thorsos, Erika Hammerschmidt, and Dawn Prince-Hughes.

Deborah elaborates on how her family directly provided her with emotional support and also enabled her to make contact with public programs designed for people with disabilities: "They want to help me as much as possible and looked into a highly rated vocational and residential program, community services for autistic adults and children" (Thorsos 2000, p.189). Deborah seems to have benefited from her family's supportive roles throughout her life, which facilitated a successful transition through childhood, adolescence, and into adulthood.

Erika credits her parents with providing emotional support throughout the developmental phases of her life: "Much of their help was simply in trying to understand my differences. From the age of four, I had a psychiatrist; from the age of ten or eleven, I went with my parents to meetings of the Tourette Syndrome Association" (Hammerschmidt 2005, p.26). Beginning at an early age, Erika's parents sought to support her becoming active in support groups for autism and Tourette's. Erika's parents appear to have set an early precedent for interacting with others who share a common disability. As she grew older, she continued to reach out to the autism community for friendship and emotional support.

Dawn felt supported by her parents, but they were uncertain about how best to help her because she was not diagnosed with autism until adulthood. Although her parents did not know she had autism, they were aware that Dawn was gay and were very supportive and proactive in response. Her parents made an effort to connect Dawn with a support group run by members of the gay and lesbian communities: "I think the other people involved cared about me and wanted to be supportive, even if at times they didn't understand me. I know they worried about my drinking as well" (Prince-Hughes 2004, p.59).

Based on her experiences coming out, had the Prince family known about Dawn's autism, they probably would have helped her reach out to other formal systems of support for people with autism. The early support of her parents enabled her to embrace her sexuality from an early age, so it seems logical that they would have supported Dawn with her autism needs in a similar fashion.

Dawn, Erika, and Deborah were born in different time periods, but shared a common experience of having supportive families who helped them reach out to broader systems of support. At the same time, a supportive family could not offset the difficulties of being undiagnosed until adulthood and the tumultuous adolescence that left Dawn homeless and addicted to alcohol. Family is important, but it is not the only factor that affects adolescent girls with autism transitioning into women.

Participation in the spiritual life of the family

Families that include girls with ASD in spiritual life and religious practice provide opportunities for social integration and generate positive feelings of self-worth (Clancy 2009; Vogel, Polloway, and Smith 2006). In this section, Temple Grandin, Deborah Thorsos, Sharon Cowhey, and Therese Ronan reflect on their adolescent experiences with organized religion. Temple and Deborah had positive experiences with religious institutions that provided opportunities for socialization and participation.

Temple was fully involved in the religious life of her family and community, just as she was included in the other activities of daily life in her household. She attributes much of her success to her mother and other family members who essentially provided her with many opportunities to practice typical social interaction:

> I had a proper religious upbringing with prayers every night, church on Sunday, and Sunday school every week. I was raised in the Episcopal Church... To my mind, all methods and demonstrations of religious ceremony were all equally valid, and I still hold this belief today. (Grandin 2006, p.222)

Temple's tolerant attitude toward religion may derive, in part, from positive feelings she experienced from being included in religious practice. Additionally, her religious observance seems to be consistent from childhood, through adolescence, and into adulthood.

Although Temple is Episcopalian and Deborah identifies as an Ashkenazi Jew, they were both included in the religious customs of their families. Their inclusion in other aspects of family life seems consistent with their participation in religious observance.

In an age before children with disabilities were regularly integrated into schools or other civic domains, Deborah was fortunate that her parents advocated for her chance to attend a Jewish day camp in Forest Hills from 1966 until 1967:

> My parents felt that since I got along well in the classroom and with typical children in my neighborhood that a summer program with regular children would work out fine for me... There were all sorts of activities, arts and crafts, swimming in the pool with group lessons, drama, and weekly cookouts at the Valley Stream Park just outside of Queens in Long Island. I got along with most of the kids, except for a few of the girls who used to tease me a lot. I liked the idea of being with typically developing children, even with some teasing going on. I adjusted to that. I've learned to ignore others who made fun of me. (Thorsos 2000, p.39)

In spite of some teasing, Deborah was thankful for the chance to interact with typically developing peers. The variety of scheduled activities at the day camp gave her a structured environment in which she could practice the vital skills of social interaction and conduct. Without the support of her parents, Deborah would not have had this important opportunity. The combination of family support coupled with participation in religious life benefited Deborah and Temple as they journeyed from childhood and made productive transitions into womanhood.

Negative experiences in religious practice

Families who exclude girls with ASD from participation in religious rites and rituals have the potential to negatively impact their developing self-esteem and sense of value (Mahoney 2005; Pargament and Raiya 2007; Webb-Mitchell 1994). This was the case for Sharon Cowhey and Therese Ronan, who became disenfranchised by their exclusion and treatment in the Catholic Church.

Sharon attended a Catholic school until she was a junior in high school when she dropped out because she was being physically reprimanded by the teachers:

> My parents never knew that the nuns would hit the kids, I would never tell them not even about my other thoughts. Mom and Dad never knew anything that I was going through and I am sure at the time they wouldn't have understood if they did. (Cowhey 2005, p.17)

Sharon's situation again demonstrates the convergence of two traditional networks of social support, family and religion, in a way that detracted from Sharon's passage into adulthood. Sharon may have been negatively impacted by the abuse she suffered at school and also the distance in her relationship with her parents. Had her parents been more in tune with her treatment in parochial school, she may have received her high school diploma. This demonstrates weaknesses in the overall support network surrounding Sharon.

Therese was not fully included in the religious life of her Catholic family. She was consistently restricted from traditional participation in Catholic rituals, starting when she was a girl and going into adulthood:

> My family didn't want me to receive my First Holy Communion in a group, because I have slow motor skills. But I was hoping that I could still dress up like a bride with a veil and walk down the aisle like my cousin Marie at her First Holy Communion. Nevertheless, I wasn't allowed to. I had to settle for a dress without a veil. I don't know why. I don't know if they knew I wanted one. (Ronan 2003, p.32)

This early restriction from an important rite of passage in the Catholic Church set a precedent for the future. Therese was deeply offended that she was not named godmother to her nephew, a high honor in the Catholic tradition:

> To this very day, I feel that I would have been just as good a godmother to the little guy. I helped to baptize him. Nevertheless, I still had no choice but to play second fiddle to his mother's sister. For the longest time, I felt that my sister-in-law was deliberately not fair and overlooked autistic me for her so-called normal sister. Now I know that if something had ever happened to them, I would be just as able to teach him the Catholic faith as her normal sister would be. (Ronan 2003, p.95)

This last passage exemplifies the ways in which traditional systems of social support, family and religion become entwined in a system that excludes and belittles women with ASD. This again demonstrates a pattern of exclusion that Therese experienced in girlhood, when she was kept from the mainstream First Communion ceremony, and continuing into adulthood when she was denied the role of godmother.

Religious practice is inextricably tied up with family life and perceptions of disability. Temple and Deborah routinely recall supportive family structures that extended into the realms of religious participation. On the other hand, Sharon and Therese often cite negative interactions with family members that overlapped with the rituals and duties of a practicing Catholic woman.

Struggling with friendships

Girls and women with ASD often report difficulties making and maintaining friendships (APA 2013; Chamberlain, Kasari, and Rotheram-Fuller 2007; Davidson 2007; Jones and Meldal 2001; Laugeson *et al.* 2009). Deborah Thorsos recognized her social limitations from an early age, but found acceptance with her siblings whom she relied on to socialize throughout her childhood: "Since I wasn't able to socialize and make friends on my own, I was dependent on my siblings for company" (Thorsos 2000, p.13).

The social support her siblings provided during childhood did not offset the difficulties that came with the expanding social terrain of adolescence. Adolescence highlighted Deborah's social shortcomings because it became obvious that her peers were developing faster: "As I entered adolescence it had become more difficult to make friends, since my autism and a short attention span made it harder to keep up with the maturing of my peers with their increasingly complex socialization" (Thorsos 2000, p.81).

Deborah describes how the characteristics of autism, a developmental disability, became more pronounced as she began adolescence. The increasingly complex nature of peer interactions and relationships became a barrier that distressed Deborah and affected her self-image: "I was aware that I wasn't as social as many of the other teenagers that I knew. I want to become more outgoing. I had difficulty initiating conversation and participating in discussions. I lack spontaneity. Any progress that I made was very slow" (Thorsos 2000, p.88).

Contrary to many stereotypes of autism, Deborah was not oblivious or unaware of the increasing social demands brought on by adolescence. Rather, her knowledge of the gaps between herself and her peers was a source of insecurity that undermined her self-esteem.

Unlike Deborah, Sharon could not rely on her siblings to provide and support a social life. Starting in childhood, Sharon struggled to maintain friendships, and this trend continued into adulthood: "Friendship never lasted too long for me," Sharon admits (2005, p.19). In the rare instances when Sharon managed to form friendships, they were short-lived: "For me socializing is out of my league. Freaky normal is the name I give to most of the people I meet" (Cowhey 2005, p.56).

Without supportive siblings to aid in building social skills, Sharon had less of a foundation to later build deeper and more meaningful friendships in adolescence and adulthood. She felt alienated from those she calls "freaky normal" people who demonstrate social fluency and have no difficulty making friends.

Erika Hammerschmidt wanted to form friendships, but had difficulty due to some of the sensory differences associated with autism. Even though she craved the company of others, she struggled to deal with the strain that interpersonal relations put on her sensory systems:

> I would become sensory-defensive. Loud noises, bright lights and strong smells raised my panic to unbearable levels. Although I didn't want to be alone, I couldn't stand being touched, or even having other people close to me. It felt like an invasion, like an attack. Sometimes my skin became so sensitive that physical contact was painful. (Hammerschmidt 2005, p.47)

Erika emotionally wanted to connect with others and to form friendships, but the physical limitations of her neurology limited her ability to engage in typical social interactions. She feels that her early sensory defensiveness limited her capacity to make friends during childhood: "Such friends were merciful exceptions to the general rule that I fit in with nobody. I am grateful to them and always will be; without their friendship, my only enjoyable interaction would have been with close family members and a few teachers" (Hammerschmidt 2005, p.128). Erika highlights the point that Deborah raised, that is, a concern about relying too heavily on family for social stimulation. Although she did not have many friends, she had the benefit of forming some early friendships with peers.

Liane Holliday Willey did not realize that it was autism that made it difficult for her to grasp the unwritten nuances of social life because she did not receive a diagnosis until adulthood. She moved through childhood and adolescence without an autism diagnosis, but struggled to master abstract social rules that came with adulthood. She wrestled with the independence that came with college life, in contrast to the comfort and ease of her high school friends whom she had known since childhood:

> I had no way of knowing that AS left me without an intrinsic awareness of what it means to make and keep friends, to fit in and mold, to work cooperatively and effectively with others. Had no way of knowing college students would be so cruel to those who did not fit in the circle of their normal. But as the first semester in college moved on, I seemed to be left behind. I noticed groups forming and all of them without me. (Holliday Willey 1999, p.42)

Without the support of her family and community where she was raised, Liane's social limitations became glaringly obvious. Before she began college, she could rely on a network of friends to tell her what was socially acceptable, but the social environment of university exposed her social shortcomings that are familiar to others with autism.

Several of the women were frustrated with their ability to initiate and maintain friendships. Deborah describes relying on her siblings to provide her with a social life she could not establish on her own. In a similar sense, Liane benefited from a supportive neighborhood and childhood friends to guide her at the beginning of her social life. However, Liane's deficits became apparent when she ventured outside the comfort of her hometown to attend a distant college. Sharon felt alienated and distant from neurotypical people beginning at an early age; her term "freaky normal" speaks to this deep discomfort and confusion surrounding mainstream, neurotypical social behavior. Erika was aware of her social limitations beginning in childhood; she was familiar with the overwhelming feelings that resulted from having atypical sensory reactions, and perhaps this early awareness empowered her to build her skill set and diminish sensory overload.

Flourishing friendships

The women reported that making friends became easier as they grew older. Therese Ronan and Erika Hammerschmidt expanded their circle of friends in high school by connecting with other students who had disabilities and shared similar interests. Erika had the added resource that internet communities of others with ASD provided, and which became an integral part of building a wide network of friends during college.

Therese utilized her segregated classroom to meet other disabled adolescents and to develop social networks based on their similar interests and placement in the education system:

> I met several new friends in my high school special education class. I met Jolie on the second day of class. I had brought some movie magazines to school to look at in my spare time. I shared one with Jolie, and we became good friends. I also met Sherry. (Ronan 2003, p.50)

Although they were in the same special ed. program, their common interest in celebrity magazines formed the basis of a strong friendship during adolescence.

Erika developed a friendship with a girl named Ali in high school that also grew out of shared interests and qualities. Both teenage girls enjoyed creating alternate worlds complete with distinct societies and social systems, and they enjoyed co-creating and interacting in these imaginary worlds. Like Erika,

Ali had been diagnosed with Asperger's syndrome, although Ali eventually identified with another diagnosis:

> What's important is that she's doing well, has a promising future and is still one of my best friends. She ended up going to the same college I went to. Through her, I've met Marie, my other kindred spirit. In some ways, she may be even more like me. (Hammerschmidt 2005, p.132)

As Erika grew older, she continued to connect with others on the autism spectrum. The internet became an instrumental method to form friends based on a shared identity and interests. Erika's early connection to others on the autism spectrum appears to have set the stage for an even wider network of friends in adulthood.

Erika praises her community of friends on the autism spectrum for their support and fellowship. Her comrades in autism further the perspective of not being alone and isolated from each other or the neurotypical human experience:

> I'm deeply grateful to have friends who have gone through some of the same difficulties I have: learning the foreign language of human life and teaching others the language of ourselves. My friends and I have come a long way, and with each other's help and the help of many other people, we've finally made Earth a place that can feel like home to us. (Hammerschmidt 2005, p.134)

Erika's comment extends beyond the realm of colloquial friendship because she is using the term "friends" to describe a community of people with autism. She speaks on behalf of her peers and elevates her personal story to a level of political representation.

Whereas Erika's social skills developed as she transitioned into adolescence, Deborah is proud of the transition she made from adolescence into adulthood. In adulthood, Deborah no longer feels isolated because of her supportive social network of friends:

> Unlike my early adolescent days when I didn't have a good network of friends outside my special school, I had established circles of friends here so I no longer felt isolated. I had the opportunity to show my folks actual proof of how I had matured over the years. (Thorsos 2000, p.283)

Deborah points to her circle of friends as a source of self-esteem and personal growth because she has struggled with friendship since childhood. She explains that she once had to rely on her family to provide a social environment in childhood, but in contrast, she is excited to demonstrate the vast circle of friends she made in adulthood, without the help of her family.

Therese, Erika, and Deborah agree that making and maintaining friendships became easier as they moved toward adulthood. Connecting with other people with disabilities proved to be an ample source of friends and support. For Therese, special education classrooms and mental health support groups helped counter some of the negative messages she received from her family about her status. Rather than internalizing messages that invalidated her status within the family, like their belief that she couldn't be a godmother or wife, she recognized the social stigma that surrounds people with disabilities. Erika successfully used the internet to build a wide circle of friends in college that satisfied her need for a social life. Further, she met her future husband through her network of friends and stayed in touch with many of these friends after graduating from college. Deborah also recognized the potential for a shared disability identity to provide greater opportunities for relationships; she also bonded with her future husband based on shared experiences of disability.

This chapter has explored the impact that families, religious affiliation, and friends have on the developmental processes of girls becoming women with autism. These social networks had the potential to either enrich or detract from the lives of these women.

CONCLUSION

This book sheds light on the experiences of baby boomer women with ASD, in particular, because six out of the seven authors were born during that era. These women were born soon after the term "autism" was coined. At that time in history, ideologies about race and disability were put into practice through institutional segregation, which was detrimental to the emotional, social, and academic development of girls with ASD. Baby boomer girls who did not have an ASD diagnosis in childhood suffered from discrimination, stigma, and social isolation. Although the political climate has shifted significantly since the baby boom, girls and women with ASD still face many of the same issues, including unemployment and poverty. Family support is critical to the success of women with ASD in every generation.

The baby boomer generation of American women with ASD grew up in an era before widespread knowledge about autism (Baron-Cohen 1997; Hacking 2009). This lack of information was exacerbated by the institutional segregation of students with disabilities. Civil rights and access to education were not ensured for baby boomer girls with ASD like Deborah Thorsos, Temple Grandin, Therese Ronan, Sharon Cowhey,

Dawn Prince-Hughes, and Liane Holliday Willey. Therese's two-year exclusion from school represents the experience of 1.75 million disabled students before 1970, who did not have the right to a free and public education (Almazan 2009). These extended absences impeded education and also deprived girls with ASD of critical time spent with peers and opportunities for social development (Goodwin and Staples 2005). The underlying ideologies that justified segregation threatened the social status and self-image of baby boomer girls with autism (Harrower and Dunlap 2001; Kasari *et al.* 2011). Deborah illustrates how internalizing ideologies of ability and able bodiedness gave rise to feelings of inferiority and difference (Almazan 2009; Dubin 2014; Gabriels and van Bourgondien 2007; McRuer 2006; Siebers 2008; Taylor and Seltzer 2010).

Dawn, Liane, and Sharon avoided segregated education because they were not diagnosed with autism during their school years, but they still struggled to form friendships and succeed in school. Dawn in particular demonstrates how undiagnosed girls and women are susceptible to problems with depression, anxiety, alcohol, relationships, and work (Wylie, Beardon, and Heath 2014). The acquisition of an ASD diagnosis provides more than a label or a means to receive services; it opens up avenues to a disability identity that affirms positive meanings of disability, pride, and connection to a wider community (Lasgaard *et al.* 2010; Portway and Johnson 2005). An ASD diagnosis allows processes of "coming home," "coming to feel we belong," "coming together," and "coming out" to begin (Gill 1997). Regardless of diagnosis, baby boomer girls with ASD faced stigma and discrimination that negatively affected developing concepts of self and society (Portway and Johnson 2005).

Like the ideologies that structure educational environments, family attitudes also shape the ways girls and women with ASD conceptualize disability and identity (Baron-Cohen 1997; Hacking 2009; Hartmann 2012; Plumb 2011). Along with an early diagnosis, financial and emotional support from their families helped Temple and Deborah graduate from high school and transition to college. The efficacy of early diagnosis and family support are magnified in light of the fact that baby boomer women with ASD grew up during an era of educational segregation (Lasgaard *et al.* 2010; Portway and Johnson 2005). Social attitudes, family values, and educational policies affect the development of girls with autism in multiple domains, including sexual development (Kelly *et al.* 2008; van Pelt 2008). Baby boomer girls with ASD were routinely separated from their peers by segregation and prejudice; therefore, they did not have equal access to sociosexual knowledge (referring to the information and meaning that children and adolescents learn from interacting with peers) (Griffith *et al.* 1999; Henault 2006; Hingsburger *et al.* 1993; Kelly *et al.* 2008; Realmuto and Ruble 1999). In addition, baby boomer women with autism confronted processes of decasualization and infantilization that limited their sexual self-expression (Garland-Thomson 2005; Gill 1996; Sandahl 2003). Like other disabled women, Therese endured efforts by her family and the state to control her sexuality and reproduction.

The socio-political system of segregation began to shift with the landmark Supreme Court ruling in *Brown vs. the Board of Education* (1954), and civil rights legislation, such as the passage of the Rehabilitation Act of 1973 and the IDEA in 1975. The dismantling of segregation and shifting ideologies presented new possibilities for the generation of American women with ASD. Generation X follows the baby boomer generation. Generation X is characterized by the acceptance of social diversity and inclusion of minorities and marginalized groups. Members of Generation X are more likely to question authority, disagree with discriminatory or unfair educational policies, and place a higher value on social relationships (Isaksen 2002; Miller 2011).

At the time this research was conducted there was only one autobiography written by an American woman with autism from Generation X. I am hesitant to draw any generalizations from one autobiography, but Erika Hammerschmidt's narrative highlights changes in the cultural climate and shifting generational values. For example, members of Generation X who have ASD benefited from the emergence of the internet. Online communities and forums allow individuals with ASD to interact without the distraction of facial expressions, body gestures, voice modulation, and other forms of nonverbal communication (Robertson 2008). The proliferation of cyber networks of people with autism offers a sense of community and belonging that was not available to baby boomer women. In addition, the internet provides people with autism with more avenues toward self-expression, political mobilization, and advocacy. The role of online social networks in the lives of women with ASD from Generation X is significant because communal attachment and a positive sense of disability identity can improve self-esteem and counter negative ideologies (Dunn and Burcaw 2013). Although political ideologies and social systems have changed due to legislation and the disability rights movement, unemployment is still an ongoing issue for women with ASD (Gabriels and van Bourgondien 2007, p.xii; Taylor and Seltzer 2010). Erika's narrative reflects how vocational rehabilitation, job training, and prejudice among employers are issues that continue to keep women with ASD from successful employment.

Effective coping techniques are vital to girls with ASD as they transition toward womanhood. My research reveals two unique strategies that helped girls with ASD move toward womanhood. Temple Grandin describes how visual symbols allowed her to feel more comfortable making important transitions in life. By visualizing various doors, she coped with the stress of the unknown. The touchstone perspective is another coping strategy that enabled Erika Hammerschmidt, Dawn Prince-Hughes, and Temple Grandin to better comprehend the social norms and practices of neurotypical society by first understanding other constellations of behavior and meaning (alien civilizations, cattle in a stockyard, and captive mountain gorillas).

In closing, the phenomena reported here are meant to help fill the gaps in the state of knowledge pertaining to how girls with autism move toward womanhood. Despite their generational differences, the unyielding support of family, financial resources, and a diagnosis in childhood appear to help girls with autism transition toward adulthood.

SEVERITY LEVELS FOR AUTISM SPECTRUM DISORDER

Security level for ASD	Social communication	Restricted interests and repetitive behaviors
Level 3: 'Requiring very substantial support'	Severe deficits in verbal and nonverbal social communication skills cause severe impairments in functioning; very limited initiation of social interactions and minimal response to social overtures from others	Preoccupations, fixated rituals and/or repetitive behaviors (RRBs) markedly interfere with functioning in all spheres. Marked distress when rituals or routines are interrupted; very difficult to redirect from fixated interest or returns to it quickly
Level 2: 'Requiring substantial support'	Marked deficits in verbal and nonverbal social communication skills; social impairments apparent even with supports in place; limited initiation of social interactions and reduced or abnormal response to social overtures from others	Rituals and repetitive behaviors (RRBs) and/or preoccupations or fixated interests appear frequently enough to be obvious to the casual observer and interfere with functioning in a variety of contexts. Distress or frustration is apparent when RRBs are interrupted; difficult to redirect from fixated interest
Level 1: 'Requiring support'	Without supports in place, deficits in social communication cause noticeable impairments. Has difficulty initiating social interactions and demonstrates clear examples of atypical or unsuccessful responses to social overtures of others. May appear to have decreased interest in social interactions	Rituals and repetitive behaviors (RRBs) cause significant interference with functioning in one or more contexts. Resists attempts by others to interrupt RRBs or to be redirected from fixated interest

Adapted from APA (2013)

APPENDIX 2

RESEARCH METHODS

Text-based qualitative methods that rely on autobiographical data are especially suited for research in autism. These autobiographies give women with ASD a voice to describe and conceptualize their own disability. Moreover, authors are provided with a venue to explain their social predicament, correct false assertions, and critique pervading scientific paradigms of autism. Since the proliferation of these narrative texts, more venues for autistic expression have emerged, namely, online communities of autistic people. Girls and women with ASD are developing networks and cyber communities to share their experiences, support each other, and redress the general public's misunderstandings.

Autobiographical testimonials of ASD upset the pathological ideology that simplifies autism as a neurological impairment with subsequent verbal, social, and behavioral deficits, rather than a complex and generative experience. When special education, occupational, physical, or ABA therapies focus on autism as pathology, the voices of students with autism are lost. Instead, educators and professionals spend time correcting or eradicating particular behaviors identified as problematic. Any subsequent research conducted in these disciplines often results in research practices that mirror and reinforce already established beliefs and practices. These preconceived beliefs manifest in the classroom and clinical settings. The absence of individuals diagnosed with autism in much of the developmental disabilities and rehabilitative literature further informs my methodological and ethical concerns. My ethical concern for the dignity, respect, and civil rights of women with ASD leads me to a qualitative, interpretive research methodology that privileges first-person narratives of autism over other types of data. Grounded theory is a research method that satisfies these ethical concerns because it demands the perspectives and voices of these women with ASD.

Grounded theory methods are used to develop a theoretical account of a topic while anchoring that account in empirical research and data (Fleischmann and Fleischmann 2012). Glaser and Strauss first explicated grounded theory in their book, *The Discovery of Grounded Theory* (1967). Strauss and Corbin (1990, p.24; see also Corbin and Strauss 1990) explain that grounded theory "is a qualitative research method that uses a systematic set of procedures to develop an inductively derived grounded theory about a phenomenon." In this approach, theory is generated through a careful reading of the data. Data informs theory, rather than data manipulated to support a given thesis. Grounded theory follows certain steps to achieve an accurate description of a phenomenon. This process can be described as an iterative process due to the switching back and forth between data collection, coding, categorizing, and theoretical validation (Jones, Quigney and Huws 2003). This flip-flopping technique of systematic comparison works well in autobiographies and other narratives that are freely submitted, not a response to a specific inquiry, so the data remains authentic and resists the influence of the research process (Jones, Zahl and Huws 2001).

Although there are several autobiographies written by women with ASD, there are few studies that utilize these accounts as data for academic research. The methodology of constant comparison was chosen for this study because it offers the voices of American women with autism an authoritative and primary position within the national discourse on autism. Furthermore, constant comparison allows themes, findings and theories to develop from the data itself. Every effort is made to avoid oversimplifying details and forcing data into pre-existing categories. As themes emerge, they are compared to findings compiled before and after, allowing the data to drive the research rather than forming preconceived hypotheses and then attempting to organize the data into those categories.

Design

The research design derives from previous studies that applied grounded theory to autobiographical materials produced by individuals with an ASD. This methodology consists of nine procedural steps:

1. Clarify the perspective and assumptions.
2. Identify a broad research question and define the key terms.
3. Set sampling criteria and collect data.
4. Data immersion, closely reading and re-reading texts and highlighting relevant passages.
5. Type up and then cut apart significant passages from the texts (data segments).
6. Question, compare, and label data segments; sort and categorize them into piles according to emerging

themes; set aside data segments that represent phenomena or categories that appear infrequently, appear insignificant, or are interesting but not relevant to the research question (open coding).

7. Continue to examine and compare categories and themes to develop tentative propositions to explain relationships, connections, and overlaps in content (axial coding).

8. Comprehensively examine propositions, develop a conceptual framework, and test the theoretical response to the research question (selective coding).

9. Write up a discussion of the findings.

Sources: Cardillo (2010); Denzin and Lincoln (1994); Fleischmann and Fleischmann (2012); Jones *et al.* (2001); Jones and Meldal (2001); Strauss and Corbin (1990, 1994, 1997)

Procedures

The research process followed general grounded theory standards (Cardillo 2010; Charmaz 2000, 2003; Denzin and Lincoln 1994; Dey 1999; Fleischmann and Fleischmann 2012; Jones *et al.* 2001; Jones and Meldal 2001; Ryan and Bernard 2003; Strauss and Corbin 1990, 1994). The first step was to clarify my perspective and consider pre-existing assumptions. In this initial stage it was important to critically think about disability studies perspectives that apply to research utilizing autobiographical materials. Second, I formed a broad research question to set the parameters of my interest in autobiographies of autism written by women and, in particular, the transition from childhood to adulthood. After posing the research question, key concepts like autism, transition, and the politics of gender were considered. Third, I collected autobiographies written by American females with autism. After collecting the autobiographies for analysis, the fourth step was immersion in the data, reading and re-reading texts, taking notes and flagging passages that dealt with relevant experiences. Due to the physical limitations of my vision impairment, I scanned all materials to create rich pdf texts that are accessible by screen reader. Fifth, Microsoft Word documents were created for each author containing notes, reviewed passages, and page numbers (data segments). Sixth, data segments were assigned labels and organized into emerging categories. For example, any commentary on romantic relationships was grouped together (open coding). In an effort to exhaust all relevant data, creating pdf files allowed me to perform keyword searches throughout all texts when a theme was raised. In other words, when the theme of romantic relationships emerged, the search terms "romance," "romantic," "relationship," "love," "boyfriend," "girlfriend," "husband," and "wife" were entered and evaluated for the contextual relevance. In the seventh phase, I compared categories and themes to propose some initial thoughts about connections, overlapping themes, and relationships between texts and authors (axial coding). The eighth step involved a holistic examination of the data in reference to the existing literature on girls with ASD transitioning toward womanhood. These findings were reviewed to develop concepts and theses based on the material (selective coding). The final step consisted of writing up the findings and conclusions based on the first eight steps.

REFERENCES

Almazan, S. (2009) 'Inclusive Education and Implications for Policy: The State of the Art and the Promise.' TASH Congressional Briefing on Inclusive Education, July 9. Accessed on 01/19/2018 at https://tash.org/wp-content/uploads/2015/07/Inclusive-Education-and-Implications-for-Policy-1.pdf

APA (American Psychiatry Association) (1994) 'Autistic Disorder.' In *Diagnostic and Statistical Manual of Mental Disorders, Fourth Edition (DSM-IV)*. Washington, DC: APA.

APA (2000) *Diagnostic and Statistical Manual of Mental Disorders, Fourth Edition, Text Revision (DSM-IV-TR)*. Washington, DC: APA.

APA (2013) *Diagnostic and Statistical Manual of Mental Disorders, Fifth Edition* (DSM-5). Lake St Louis, MO: APA.

Baio, J. (2014) 'Prevalence of Autism Spectrum Disorder among children aged 8 years—Autism and Developmental Disabilities Monitoring Network, 11 sites.' *2010 Surveillance Summaries* March 28, 63, SS02, 1–21.

Barnhill, A.C. (2007) *At Home in the Land of Oz: Autism, My Sister, and Me*. London: Jessica Kingsley Publishers.

Baron-Cohen, S. (1997) *Mindblindness: An Essay on Autism and Theory of Mind*. Cambridge, MA: MIT Press.

Barron, S. with Barron, J. (1992) *There's a Boy in Here: Emerging from the Bonds of Autism*. New York: Avon Books.

Beavers, D.J. (1982) *Autism: Nightmare without End*. Port Washington, NY: Ashley Books.

Begeer, S., Mandell, D., Wijnker-Holmes, B., Venderbosch, S., Rem, D., Stekelenburg, F. and Koot, H.M. (2013) 'Sex differences in the timing of identification among children and adults with autism spectrum disorders.' *Journal of Autism and Developmental Disorders 43*(5), 1151–1156.

Bettelheim, B. (1967) *The Empty Fortress: Infantile Autism and the Birth of the Self.* New York: Free Press.

Bleuler, E. (2010) 'Dementia praecox or the group of schizophrenias.' *Vertex (Buenos Aires, Argentina) 21*(93), 394–400.

Block, P. (2000) 'Sexuality, fertility and danger—Twentieth-century images of women with cognitive disabilities.' *Sexuality and Disability 18*(4), 239–254.

Bracher, M. (2013) 'Living without a Diagnosis—Formations of Pre-diagnostic Identity in the Lives of AS People Diagnosed in Adulthood.' Doctoral dissertation, University of Southampton.

Brooks, W.T. and Benson, B. (2014) 'Gender Differences in Social Skills, Peer Relationships, and Emotional Correlates in Adults with High Functioning Autism Spectrum Disorders.' OhioLINK Electronic Theses and Dissertations Center, Ohio State University.

Buizer-Voskamp, J.E., Laan, W., Staal, W.G., Hennekam, E.A., Aukes, M.F., Termorshuizen, F. *et al.* (2011) 'Paternal age and psychiatric disorders: Findings from a Dutch population registry.' *Schizophrenia Research 129*(2), 128–132.

Bumiller, K. (2008) 'Quirky citizens: Autism, gender, and reimagining disability.' *Signs: Journal of Women in Culture and Society 33*(4), 967–991.

Cardillo, L.W. (2010) 'Empowering narratives: Making sense of the experience of growing up with chronic illness or disability.' *Western Journal of Communication 74*(5), 525–546.

Carley, M.J. (2008) *Asperger's from the Inside Out: A Supportive and Practical Guide for Anyone with Asperger's Syndrome.* New York: TarcherPerigree.

Chamberlain, B., Kasari, C. and Rotheram-Fuller, E. (2007) 'Involvement or isolation? The social networks of children with autism in regular classrooms.' *Journal of Autism and Developmental Disorders 37*(2), 230–242.

Charlton, J.I. (1998) *Nothing About Us Without Us: Disability, Oppression and Empowerment.* Berkeley, CA: University of California Press.

Charmaz, K. (2000) 'Experiencing Chronic Illness.' In G.L. Albrecht, R. Fitzpatrick, and S.C. Scrimshaw (eds) *The Handbook of Social Studies in Health and Medicine* (pp.277–292). London, UK: Sage.

Charmaz, K. (2003) 'Strategies for Qualitative Inquiry.' In N.K. Denzin and Y.S. Lincoln (eds) *Grounded Theory: Objectivist and Constructivist Methods* (pp.249–291). Thousand Oaks, CA: Sage.

Christensen, D.L., Baio, J., van Naarden Braun, K., Bilder, D., Charles, J., Constantino, J.N. *et al.* (2016) 'Centers for Disease Control and Prevention (CDC): Prevalence and characteristics of autism spectrum disorder among children aged 8 years—Autism and Developmental Disabilities Monitoring Network, 11 sites, United States, 2012.' *MMWR Surveillance Summaries 65*(3), 1–23.

Christopher, K. (2003) 'Autistic boy killed during exorcism.' *Skeptical Inquirer 27*(6), Nov/Dec, 11. Committee for the Scientific Investigation of Claims of the Paranormal (SCICOP).

Clancy, M. (2009) 'Inclusion identifies the meaning of church for a parent.' *Journal of Religion, Disability & Health 13*(3–4), 334–338.

Clifford, S., Dissanayake, C., Bui, Q.M., Huggins, R., Taylor, A.K. and Loesch, D.Z. (2007) 'Autism spectrum phenotype in males and females with fragile X full mutation and premutation.' *Journal of Autism and Developmental Disorders 37*(4), 738–747.

Corbin, J.M. and Strauss, A. (1990) 'Grounded theory research: Procedures, canons, and evaluative criteria.' *Qualitative Sociology 13*(1), 3–21.

Couser, G.T. (2007) 'Undoing hardship: Life writing and disability law.' *Narrative 15*, 1, January, Ohio State University.

Couser, G.T. (2009) *Signifying Bodies: Disability in Contemporary Life Writing*. Ann Arbor, MI: University of Michigan Press.

Cowhey, S.P. (2005) *Going through the Motions: Coping with Autism*. PublishAmerica.

Davidson, J. (2007) '"In a world of her own..." Re-presenting alienation and emotion in the lives and writings of women with autism.' *Gender, Place & Culture 14*(6), 659–677.

DeMatteo, F.J., Arter, P.S., Sworen-Parise, C., Fasciana, M. and Paulhamus, M.A. (2012) 'Social skills training for young adults with Autism Spectrum Disorder: Overview and implications for practice.' *National Teacher Education Journal 5*(4), 57–65.

Denzin, N.K. and Lincoln, Y.S. (1994) *Handbook of Qualitative Research*. London, UK: Sage.

Dey, I. (1999) *Grounding Grounded Theory: Guidelines for Qualitative Inquiry*. San Diego, CA: Academic Press.

Dubin, N. (2014) *The Autism Spectrum and Depression*. London: Jessica Kingsley Publishers.

Dunn, D.S. and Burcaw, S. (2013) 'Disability identity: Exploring narrative accounts of disability.' *Rehabilitation Psychology 58*(2), 148–157.

Durkin, M.S., Maenner, M.J., Newschaffer, C.J., Lee, L.C., Cunniff, C.M., Daniels, J.L. *et al.* (2008) 'Advanced parental age and the risk of autism spectrum disorder.' *American Journal of Epidemiology 168*(11), 1268–1276.

Dworzynski, K., Ronald, A., Bolton, P. and Happé, F. (2012) 'How different are boys and girls above and below the diagnostic threshold for autism spectrum disorders?' *Journal of the American Academy of Child and Adolescent Psychiatry 51*(8), 788–797.

Ferguson, S. (producer) and Jackson, M. (dir.) (2010) *Temple Grandin*. HBO.

Fleischmann, A. and Fleischmann, R.H. (2012) 'Advantages of an ADHD diagnosis in adulthood: Evidence from online narratives.' *Qualitative Health Research 22*(11), 1486–1496.

Frazier, T.W., Georgiades, S., Bishop, S.L. and Hardan, A.Y. (2014) 'Behavioral and cognitive characteristics of females and males with autism in the Simons Simplex Collection.' *Journal of the American Academy of Child and Adolescent Psychiatry 53*(3), 329–340.

Freedman, A.M., Ebin, E.V. and Wilson, E. (1962) 'Autistic schizophrenic children: An experiment in the use of D-lysergic acid diethylamide (LSD 25).' *Archives of General Psychiatry 6*, March. Chicago, IL: American Medical Association.

Gabriels, R.L. and van Bourgondien, M.E. (2007) 'Sexuality and Autism. Individual, Family and Community Perspectives and Interventions.' In R.L. Gabriels and D.E. Hill (eds) *Growing Up with Autism: Working with School-age Children and Adolescents* (pp.58–72). New York: Guilford Publications.

Garland-Thomson, R. (2005) 'Feminist disability studies.' *Signs 30*(2), 1557–1587.

Gill, C.J. (1996) 'Dating and relationship issues.' *Sexuality and Disability 14*(3), 183–190.

Gill, C.J. (1997) 'Four types of integration in disability identity development.' *Journal of Vocational Rehabilitation 9*(1), 39–46.

Gill, C.J. (2001) 'Divided Understandings.' In G.L. Albrecht, K. Seelman, and M. Bury (eds) *Handbook of Disability Studies* (pp.351–373). London, UK: Sage.

Glaser, B.G. and Strauss, A.L. (1967) *The Discovery of Grounded Theory: Strategies for Qualitative Research*. New York: Transaction Publishers.

Goodwin, D.L. and Staples, K. (2005) 'The meaning of summer camp experiences to youths with disabilities.' *Adapted Physical Activity Quarterly 22*(2), 160–178.

Gougeon, N.A. (2010) 'Sexuality and autism: A critical review of selected literature using a social-relationship model of disability.' *American Journal of Sexuality Education 5*, 328–351.

Grandin, T. (2006) *Thinking in Pictures: And Other Reports from My Life with Autism.* New York: Vintage Books.

Grandin, T. and Scariano, M.M. (1986) *Emergence: Labeled Autistic.* Novato, CA: Arena Press Books.

Grealy, L. (1994) *Autobiography of a Face.* New York: Houghton-Mifflin.

Griffith, E.M., Pennington, B.F., Wehner, E.A. and Rogers, S.J. (1999) 'Executive functions in young children with autism.' *Child Development 70*(4), 817–832.

Grinker, R.R. (2007) *Unstrange Minds: Remapping the World of Autism.* New York: Basic Books.

Guber, P. and Peters, J. (producers) and Levinson, B. (dir.) (1988) *Rain Man* [Film]. MGM.

Hacking, I. (2009) 'Autistic autobiography.' *Philosophical Transactions of the Royal Society B: Biological Sciences 364*, 1522, 1467–1473. Accessed on 01/12/2018 at http://doi.org/10.1098/rstb.2008.0329

Hall, A. (2015) *Literature and Disability.* London, UK: Routledge.

Hammerschmidt, E. (2005) *Born on the Wrong Planet.* Palo Alto, CA: Tyborne Hill.

Harrower, J.K. and Dunlap, G. (2001) 'Including children with autism in general education classrooms: A review of effective strategies.' *Behavior Modification 25*(5), 762–784.

Hartmann, A. (2012) *Autism and Its Impact on Families.* Master of Social Work Clinical Research Papers 35. Accessed on 07/02/2018 at http://sophia.stkate.edu/msw_papers/35

Head, A.M., McGillivray, J.A. and Stokes, M.A. (2014) 'Gender differences in emotionality and sociability in children with autism spectrum disorders.' *Molecular Autism 5*(19).

Henault, I. (2006) *Asperger's Syndrome and Sexuality: From Adolescence through Adulthood.* London: Jessica Kingsley Publishers.

Hiller, R.M., Young, R.L. and Weber, N. (2014) 'Sex differences in autism spectrum disorder based on DSM-5 criteria: Evidence from clinician and teacher reporting.' *Journal of Abnormal Child Psychology 42*(8), 1381–1393.

Hingsburger, D., Tremblay, D., Gagnon, M.L., Hénault, I. and Mitelman, S. (1993) *Parents Ask Questions about Sexuality and Children with Developmental Disabilities.* Vancouver, BC, Canada: Family Support Institute Press.

Hockenberry, J. (1995) *Moving Violations*. New York: Hyperion.

Holliday Willey, L. (1999) *Pretending to be Normal: Living with Asperger's Syndrome*. London: Jessica Kingsley Publishers.

Hu-Lince, D., Craig, D.W., Huentelman, M.J. and Stephan, D.A. (2005) 'The Autism Genome Project.' *American Journal of PharmacoGenomics 5*(4), 233–246.

Isaksen, J.L. (2002) 'Generation X.' *St James Encyclopedia of Pop Culture*.

Jamain, S., Quach, H., Betancur, C., Råstam, M., Colineaux, C., Gillberg, I.C. and Bourgeron, T. (2003) 'Mutations of the X-linked genes encoding neuroligins NLGN3 and NLGN4 are associated with autism.' *Nature Genetics 34*(1), 27–29.

Jones, R.S.P. and Meldal, T.O. (2001) 'Social relationships and Asperger's syndrome: A qualitative analysis of first-hand accounts.' *Journal of Learning Disabilities 5*(1), 35–41.

Jones, R.S.P., Quigney, C. and Huws, J. (2003) 'First-hand accounts of sensory perceptual experiences in autism: A qualitative analysis.' *Journal of Intellectual & Developmental Disability 28*(2), 112–121.

Jones, R.S.P., Zahl, A. and Huws, J.C. (2001) 'First-hand accounts of emotional experiences in autism: A qualitative analysis.' *Disability & Society 16*(3), 393–401.

Kanner, L. (1943) 'Autistic disturbances of affective contact.' *Nervous Child 2*, 217–250.

Kapp, S.K., Gillespie-Lynch, K., Sherman, L.E. and Hutman, T. (2013) 'Deficit, difference, or both? Autism and neurodiversity.' *Developmental Psychology 49*(1), 59.

Karasik, P. and Karasik, J. (2003) *The Ride Together: A Brother and Sister's Memoir of Autism in the Family*. New York: Washington Square Press.

Kasari, C., Locke, J., Gulsrud, A. and Rotheram-Fuller, E. (2011) 'Social networks and friendships at school: Comparing children with and without ASD.' *Journal of Autism and Developmental Disorders 41*, 5, 533–544.

Kearns-Bodkin, J.N. and Leonard, K.E. (2008) 'Relationship functioning among adult children of alcoholics.' *Journal of Studies on Alcohol and Drugs 69*(6), 941–950.

Keller, H. (1903) *The Story of My Life*. New York: Doubleday, Page & Co.

Kelly, A.B., Garnett, M.S., Attwood, T. and Peterson, C. (2008) 'Autism spectrum symptomatology in children: The impact of family and peer relationships.' *Journal of Abnormal Child Psychology 36*(7), 1069.

Koller, R. (2001) 'Sexuality and adolescents with autism.' *Sexuality and Disability 18*(2), 125–135.

Krahn, T.M.M. (2012) 'The extreme male brain theory of autism and the potential adverse effects for boys and girls with autism.' *Journal of Bioethical Inquiry 9*(1), 93–103.

Lasgaard, M., Nielsen, A., Eriksen, M.E. and Goossens, L. (2010) 'Loneliness and social support in adolescent boys with autism spectrum disorders.' *Journal of Autism and Developmental Disorders 40*(2), 218–226.

Laugeson, E.A., Frankel, F., Mogil, C. and Dillon, A.R. (2009) 'Parent-assisted social skills training to improve friendships in teens with autism spectrum disorders.' *Journal of Autism and Developmental Disorders 39*(4), 596–606.

Lennon, R. and Eisenberg, N. (1987) 'Gender and Age Differences in Empathy and Sympathy.' In N. Eisenberg and J. Strayer (eds) *Cambridge Studies in Social and Emotional Development. Empathy and its Development* (pp.195–217). New York: Cambridge University Press.

Levy, S.E., Giarelli, E., Lee, L.C., Schieve, L.A., Kirby, R.S., Cunniff, C. *et al.* (2010) 'Autism spectrum disorder and co-occurring developmental, psychiatric, and medical conditions among children in multiple populations of the United States.' *Journal of Developmental & Behavioral Pediatrics 31*(4), 267–275.

Lovaas, O.I. (1966) 'A program for the establishment of speech in psychotic children.' In J.K. Wing (ed.) *Early Childhood Autism* (pp.115–144). London, UK: Pergamon Press.

Mahoney, A. (2005) 'Religion and conflict in marital and parent–child relationships.' *Journal of Social Issues 61*(4), 689–706.

Mandy, W., Murin, M. and Skuse, D. (2015) 'The Cognitive Profile in Autism Spectrum Disorders.' In M. Leboyer and P Chaste (eds) *Autism Spectrum Disorders: Phenotypes, Mechanisms and Treatments* (Vol. 180) (pp.34–45). Basel, Switzerland: Karger Publishers.

Martin, N., Beardon, L., Hodge, N., Goodley, D. and Madriaga, M. (2008) 'Towards an inclusive environment for university students who have Asperger syndrome (AS).' *The Journal of Inclusive Practice in Further and Higher Education 1*(1), 3–14.

Mattingly, C. and Lawlor, M. (2000) 'Learning from stories: Narrative interviewing in cross-cultural research.' *Scandinavian Journal of Occupational Therapy 7*(1), 4–14.

Mayes, S.D., Calhoun, S.L., Murray, M.J. and Zahid, J. (2011) 'Variables associated with anxiety and depression in children with autism.' *Journal of Developmental and Physical Disabilities 23*(4), 325–337.

McDonnell, J. (1993) *News from the Border: A Mother's Memoir of Her Autistic Son*. With an Afterword by Paul McDonnell. New York: Ticknor & Fields.

McRuer, R. (2006) *Crip Theory: Cultural Signs of Queerness and Disability*. New York: New York University Press.

Meadan, H., Halle, J.W. and Ebata, A.T. (2010) 'Families with children who have autism spectrum disorders: Stress and support.' *Exceptional Children 77*(1), 7–36.

Mehzabin, P. and Stokes, M.A. (2011) 'Self-assessed sexuality in young adults with high-functioning autism.' *Research in Autism Spectrum Disorders 5*, 614–621.

Miedzianik, D. (1986) *My Autobiography*. Ireland: University of Nottingham.

Miller, J. (2011) *The Generation X Report: Active, Balanced, and Happy: These Young Americans Are Not Bowling Alone*. Longitudinal Study of American Youth – University of Michigan. p.1. Accessed on 05/29/2013 at http://home.isr.umich.edu/files/2011/10/GenX_Report_Fall2011.pdf

Mitchell, D.T. and Snyder, S.L. (2000) *Narrative Prosthesis: Disability and the Dependencies of Discourse*. Ann Arbor, MI: University of Michigan Press.

Muhle, R., Trentacoste, S.V. and Rapin, I. (2004) 'The genetics of autism.' *Pediatrics 113*(5), e472–e486.

O'Neill, J.L. (1999) *Through the Eyes of Aliens: A Book about Autistic People*. London: Jessica Kingsley Publishers.

Pargament, K.I. and Raiya, H.A. (2007) 'A decade of research on the psychology of religion and coping: Things we assumed and lessons we learned.' *Psyke & logos 28*(2), 25.

Park, C.C. (1982) *The Siege: The First Eight Years of an Autistic Child. With an Epilogue, Fifteen Years After*. Boston, MA: Little, Brown & Company.

Patterson, K. and Hughes, B. (1999) 'Disability studies and phenomenology: The carnal politics of everyday life.' *Disability & Society 14*, 5.

Plumb, J.C. (2011) 'The Impact of Social Support and Family Resilience on Parental Stress in Families with a Child Diagnosed with an Autism Spectrum Disorder.' Doctorate in Social Work (DSW) Dissertations. Accessed on 07/02/2018 at https://repository.upenn.edu/edissertations_sp2/14

Portway, S.M. and Johnson, B. (2005) 'Do you know I have Asperger's syndrome? Risks of a non-obvious disability.' *Health, Risk and Society 7*(1), 73–83.

Prince-Hughes, D. (2002) *Aquamarine Blue 5: Personal Stories of College Students with Autism*. Athens, OH: Swallow Press/Ohio University Press.

Prince-Hughes, D. (2004) *Songs of the Gorilla Nation: My Journey through Autism*. New York: Harmony Books.

Radical Neurodivergence Speaking (no date) Accessed on 07/02/2018 at timetolisten.blogspot.com/

Realmuto, G.M. and Ruble, L.A. (1999) 'Sexual behaviors in autism: Problems of definition and management.' *Journal of Autism and Developmental Disorders 29*(2), 121–127.

Renty, J.O and Roeyers, H. (2006) 'Satisfaction with formal support and education for children with autism spectrum disorder: The voices of the parents.' *Child: Care, Health and Development 32*(3), 371–385.

Robertson, S.M. (2008) 'Autistic acceptance, the college campus, and technology: Growth of neurodiversity in society and academia.' *Disability Studies Quarterly 28*(4).

Ronan, T.M. (2003) *Therese's World*. Bloomington, IN: Xlibris Corporation.

Rose, I. (2005) 'Autistic Autobiography: Introducing the Field.' In *Proceedings of the Autism and Representation: Writing, Cognition, Disability Conference* (Vol. 12). Accessed on 07/02/2018 at http://case.edu/affil/sce/Representing%20Autism.html

Ryan, G.W. and Bernard, H.R. (2003) 'Techniques to identify themes.' *Field Methods 15*(1), 85–109.

Sandahl, C. (2003) 'Queering the crip or cripping the queer? Intersections of queer and crip identities in solo autobiographical performance.' *GLQ: A Journal of Lesbian and Gay Studies 9*(1), 25–56.

Schneider, E. (1999) *Discovering My Autism: Apologia Pro Vita Sua (with Apologies to Cardinal Newman)*. London: Jessica Kingsley Publishers.

Shore, S.M. (2003) *Beyond the Wall: Personal Experiences with Autism and Asperger Syndrome*. Shawnee, KS: AAPC Publishing.

Siebers, T. (2008) *Disability Theory*. Ann Arbor, MI: University of Michigan Press.

Simone, R. and Holliday Willey, L. (2010) *Aspergirls: Empowering Females with Asperger Syndrome*. London: Jessica Kingsley Publishers.

Snyder, S.L. and Mitchell, D.T. (2002) 'Out of the ashes of eugenics: Diagnostic regimes in the United States and the making of a disability minority.' *Patterns of Prejudice 36*(1), 79–103.

Snyder, S.L. and Mitchell, D.T. (2010) *Cultural Locations of Disability*. Chicago, IL: University of Chicago Press.

Solomon, M., Miller, M., Taylor, S.L., Hinshaw, S.P. and Carter, C.S. (2012) 'Autism symptoms and internalizing psychopathology in girls and boys with autism spectrum disorders.' *Journal of Autism and Developmental Disorders 42*(1), 48–59.

Stanghellini, G. (2001) 'A dialectical conception of autism.' *Philosophy, Psychiatry, & Psychology 8*(4), 295–298.

Stone, H. (2005) 'Autism.' In G. Albrecht (ed.) *Encyclopedia of Disability*. Thousand Oaks, CA: Sage Publications.

Strauss, A. and Corbin, J.M. (1990) *Basics of Qualitative Research: Grounded Theory Procedures and Techniques*. Thousand Oaks, CA: Sage Publications, Inc.

Strauss, A. and Corbin, J.M. (1994) 'Grounded Theory Methodology.' In N.K. Denzin and Y.S. Lincoln (eds) *Handbook of Qualitative Research* (pp.273–285). Thousand Oaks, CA: Sage.

Strauss, A. and Corbin, J.M. (1997) *Grounded Theory in Practice*. Thousand Oaks, CA: Sage.

Taylor, J.L. and Seltzer, M.M. (2010) 'Changes in the behavioral phenotype during the transition to adulthood.' *Journal of Autism and Developmental Disorders 40*(12), 1431–1446.

Thorsos, D.I. (2000) *Sour Sweet: Adversity into Creativity*. Renton, WA: First Word Publishing.

Tissot, C. (2009) 'Establishing a sexual identity: Case studies of learners with autism and learning difficulties.' *Autism 13*(6), 551–566.

van Pelt, J. (2008) 'Autism into adulthood—Making the transition.' *Social Work Today 8*(5), 12.

Vogel, J., Polloway, E.A. and Smith, J.D. (2006) 'Inclusion of people with mental retardation and other developmental disabilities in communities of faith.' *Mental Retardation 44*(2), 100–111.

Walker, N. (2014) 'Neurodiversity: Some basic terms & definitions.' [Online] Neurocosmopolitanism, September 27. Accessed on 02/07/2018 at http://neurocosmopolitanism.com/neurodiversity-some-basic-terms-definitions/

Walker, N. (2015) 'Neuroqueer: An introduction.' [Online] Neurocosmopilitanism, May 2. Accessed on 07/02/2018 at http://neurocosmopolitanism.com/neuroqueer-an-introduction/

Webb-Mitchell, B. (1994) 'The spiritual abuse of people with disabilities.' *Journal of Religion in Disability & Rehabilitation 2*(1), 55–63.

Wylie, P., Beardon, L. and Heath, S. (2014) *Very Late Diagnosis of Asperger Syndrome (Autism Spectrum Disorder): How Seeking a Diagnosis in Adulthood Can Change Your Life*. London: Jessica Kingsley Publishers.

Yergeau, M. (2013) 'Clinically significant disturbance: On theorists who theorize theory of mind.' *Disability Studies Quarterly 33*(4).

Yergeau, M. (2017) *Authoring Autism: On Rhetoric and Neurological Queerness*. Durham, NC: Duke University Press.

Zola, I. (1982) *Missing Pieces*. Philadelphia, PA: Temple University Press.

SUBJECT INDEX

AUTHOR INDEX